BLUEPRINT

Maths
Teacher's
Resource Book
Key Stage 1

Wendy and David Clemson

Second edition

Stanley Thornes (Publishers) Ltd

Do you receive *BLUEPRINTS NEWS*?

Blueprints is an expanding series of practical teacher's ideas books and photocopiable resources for use in primary schools. Books are available for separate infant and junior age ranges for every core and foundation subject, as well as for an ever widening range of other primary teaching needs. These include **Blueprints Primary English** books and **Blueprints Resource Banks**. **Blueprints** are carefully structured around the demands of the National Curriculum in England and Wales, but are used successfully by schools and teachers in Scotland, Northern Ireland and elsewhere.

Blueprints provide:

- *Total curriculum coverage*
- *Hundreds of practical ideas*
- *Books specifically for the age range you teach*
- *Flexible resources for the whole school or for individual teachers*
- *Excellent photocopiable sheets – ideal for assessment and children's work profiles*
- *Supreme value.*

Books may be bought by credit card over the telephone and information obtained on **(01242) 577944**. Alternatively, photocopy and return this **FREEPOST** form to receive **Blueprints News**, our regular update on all new and existing titles. You may also like to add the name of a friend who would be interested in being on the mailing list.

Please add my name to the **BLUEPRINTS NEWS** mailing list.

Mr/Mrs/Miss/Ms _____

Home address _____

_____ Postcode _____

School address _____

_____ Postcode _____

Please also send **BLUEPRINTS NEWS** to:

Mr/Mrs/Miss/Ms _____

Address _____

_____ Postcode _____

To: Marketing Services Dept., Stanley Thornes Ltd, FREEPOST (GR 782), Cheltenham, GL50 1BR

Text © Wendy and David Clemson 1992
Original line illustrations by Tim Smith © ST(P) Ltd 1992

First published in 1992 by:
Stanley Thornes (Publishers) Ltd
Ellenborough House
Wellington Street
CHELTENHAM GL50 1YW
England

Reprinted 1993

Second edition 1995

Reprinted 1995

A catalogue record for this book is available from the British Library.

ISBN 0–7487–2206–8

Typeset by Tech-Set, Gateshead, Tyne & Wear.
Printed and bound in Great Britain at The Bath Press, Avon.

CONTENTS

Introduction

In order to be able to extract meaning from the world around us it is essential that we become numerate, just as we need to be literate and able to deploy language in a variety of ways. Both natural and designed environments are explicable in some respects only through mathematics. To be deprived of the skills necessary to understand the constants and variables in the world is to be both intellectually and practically disadvantaged. It is therefore vitally important that all children are exposed to the challenge, beauty, relevance and breadth of mathematics. But to communicate all this demands enlivening teaching and learning.

Mathematicians in the making need enthusiastic mathematicians as teachers. If you yourself find maths the most irksome part of the curriculum, please give it another go! Mathematics is essentially about pattern. Human beings search for patterns in experience in order to understand the world. Mathematics unites language and science. Mathematics is not a 'way of thinking' independent of language, but a realisation that mathematics is pattern enriches thinking and understanding. Mathematics also engages us in the measurement of shapes, spaces and comparisons.

To measure is to try to obtain some information about the environment. We attempt to describe the passing of time through the use of regular intervals, and we produce scale maps of road systems. We offer for sale products which can be compared in terms of their size and quantity, and national economies are geared to the quantity of raw materials and the cost of turning these materials into artifacts. Measurement is at the heart of civilisation.

If every child leaves your class able to construct and read a block graph, for example, they are *all* on the way to becoming competent mathematicians, and that is something you can take credit for and be proud of. Whatever the future of the nation, simply by looking at ways of interpreting data you will have influenced some of the lives of the children with whom you have worked. Never underestimate the capabilities of young children, the power of mathematics or the influence of the teacher!

WHAT IS BLUEPRINTS MATHS?

Blueprints Maths is a practical, teacher's resource specifically written to fulfil the requirements of the National Curriculum in maths for primary schools. It is intended for all teachers, particularly those who are not maths specialists, and provides comprehensive coverage in an easy-to-follow format. *Blueprints Maths* is a rich resource of practical ideas to use alongside other materials within your scheme of work. It gives children meaningful, relevant things to do. *Blueprints Maths Key Stage 1* provides activities for 5–7 year olds; *Blueprints Maths Key Stage 2* provides activities for 7–11 year olds. For each key stage there is a *Teacher's Resource Book* and a book of *Pupils' Copymasters*.

The *Teacher's Resource Book* and the accompanying *Pupils' Copymasters* follow closely the structure of the *Mathematics in the National Curriculum (1995)*. The *Teacher's Resource Book* is arranged in sections, each corresponding to part of the National Curriculum Programme of Study. The *Pupils' Copymasters* match the activities in the *Teacher's Resource Book*.

The *Blueprints Maths Key Stage 1 Teacher's Resource Book* provides dozens of lively activities through Key Stage 1. The book is arranged in two main sections, each relating to work expected of children through this Key Stage, covering Attainment Targets 2 and 3, at Levels 1–3. A discussion about how to cover 'Using and applying mathematics' appears at the front of the book. At the start of each part of the book there is an extract from the Statutory Orders, comprising the appropriate part of the Programme of Study.

The *Teacher's Resource Book* will prove an invaluable resource, even without the use of the pupils' copymasters. You can, in developing your own schemes of work, choose activities to fit those aspects on which you are focusing. There is a record sheet at the back of the book, on which you can identify activities the children have tried, and also note work done contributing to 'Using and applying mathematics'.

The *Pupils' Copymasters* book provides 113 photo-copiable worksheets. C1–C101 are linked specifically to many of the activities in the *Teacher's Resource Book*. R1–R11 are resource copymasters and can be used again and again across all sections of the book. When completed, the worksheets can be added to the children's workfiles or used as exemplar material in pupil profiles. They may also be seen as a resource for teacher assessment. There is a tick list at the back of the book, on which you can note the photocopy sheets the children have made use of.

Blueprints Maths Key Stage 1 provides coverage of Attainment Targets 2 and 3 for Levels 1–3. It is expected that most children should master Level 2 but Level 3 work is provided for those children who require work beyond Level 2.

The *Pupils' Copymasters* are provided as support for busy teachers and to provide a framework for recording the children's achievement.

Using and applying mathematics

'Using and applying mathematics' has been treated differently from the other parts of the Programme of Study. At the beginning of the book you will find a brief summary of how you can incorporate work on 'Using and applying mathematics' into the activities the children do.

Record keeping

There are photocopiable record sheets at the back of the *Teacher's Resource Book* and the *Pupils' Copymasters* book. Photocopy one *Teacher's Resource Book* record sheet per child and write in comments on the Levels of the appropriate ATs the child has worked at. Photocopy one *Pupils' Copymaster* record sheet per child and tick the photocopy sheets each child has worked on.

How to use this book

This book has been tied to the National Curriculum Programme of Study so that you can assess the activities easily. Within each of the sections:

- Number
- Shape, space and measures

the activities have been arranged to match points in the Programme of Study with Level 1 activities first, and so on.

At the beginning is a discussion of how to achieve coverage of 'Using and applying mathematics', which demands a different treatment in that it 'threads through' the other parts of the Programme of Study.

Our intention is not that the activities should be worked through in linear fashion. We hope that you will dip into the book and use the activities where they are appropriate. We would favour an approach where, for a period of time, which may be a day or weeks, you involve all the children in activities in, for example, 'Number',

at whatever Levels they are working. The activities will also support thematic work where a number of curriculum areas are involved at the same time. For example, the shape and space activities would enhance, and themselves be enhanced by, work in art, PE and music.

At the end of the book you will find a record sheet, which will enable you to register a child's contact with work on each Attainment Target at a Level.

If you also have the *Pupils' Copymasters* use them to support learning and help with consolidation, assessment and evaluation where appropriate. You will find the copymasters referred to in this book with the

symbol:

Copymasters 1–101 are tied to activities in number and shape, space, and measures. **Copymasters R1–R11** can be used again and again as general resources across all the sections of the book.

RESOURCING YOUR MATHEMATICS

Most of the resources you and the children need for mathematics are commonly and readily available. In the activities in each section we assume you have such things as pots and containers, collections of objects, and so on; these general resources are listed below. At the beginning of each section, you will find suggestions for additions to the general resources that will help in working in that particular section.

In addition to the children themselves, you will need a resource bank in the classroom, easily accessible to you and preferably also to the children. Pencils, crayons, books, rulers and the like are in most class-rooms. Some of these can be set aside as maths resources, for the time that they are needed. Some commercially produced counting aids, like Unifix®, Colour Factor®, Cuisenaire®, Multilink® and Centicubes® are commonly available in most schools and are extremely useful. Here are some suggestions for other possible resources:

- Beads, conkers and other nuts, shells, marbles, sticks, timber offcuts, wooden blocks, cotton reels, pressed and mounted leaves, seeds, feathers, egg cups, spoons, soft toys, model farm animals, dolls' house furniture and dolls, model cars, socks, balls of wool, spent matches, elastic bands, pebbles and pieces of string, heavy rope, skipping rope

- Containers, cartons and boxes of all kinds, jugs, beakers, jars and plastic bottles, tins, yogurt pots, margarine tubes, matchboxes, food boxes, egg boxes and boxes big enough for children to get into
- Marbles, beads, dice and spinners
- Building bricks, Duplo®, Lego®, Plasticine®, clay, play dough (see opposite) and 'play food' or other items made with this, drinking straws and Artstraws®
- Pictures from magazines and catalogues, old greeting cards and postcards
- Number lines, play money, metre sticks, cardboard clock face; rubber stamps with pictures, numbers, coins or shapes on them; number games, calculators
- Fabrics, metal objects and samples of natural materials
- A wide variety of art materials, including a range of varieties of paper, cardboard, gummed shapes, scissors, sticky tape, chalks, brushes, paints and inks.

In addition to these general resources we have found some further items of particular value. These are:

- Blank dice, which can be bought through educational suppliers, and can be written on with felt-tip pen, or have stick-on numerals attached
- Many-sided dice, obtainable from shops selling elaborate board games

● Play dough, which can be made as follows: Stir together 2 cups unsifted flour, 1 cup salt, 1 cup (approximately) water and 2 tablespoons cooking oil. This recipe comes from *The Playgroup Book* by Marie Winn and Mary Ann Porcher. Experiment with the proportions until the consistency is such that it holds its shape. Play dough can be hardened by placing models in a low-temperature oven to dry out. It then takes powder paint well and can be varnished. If you want a batch of, for example, badges or fruits of one colour, food colouring can be added with the water when the dough is made up.

BOOKS ▶

Books are also necessary. We enclose a starter list of children's books here, which we have drawn up with the help of *Books for Infant Mathematics*, produced by the Association of Teachers of Mathematics.

Story books

Ahlberg, A. and J., *Burglar Bill*, Heinemann/Mammoth

Anno, M., *Anno's Flea Market*, Bodley Head

Berenstein, S. and J., *Inside, Outside, Upside Down*, Collins

Blake, Q., *Mister Magnolia*, J Cape

Briggs, R., *Jim and the Beanstalk*, Picture Puffin

Burningham, J., *The Shopping Basket*, J Cape

Carle, E., *The Very Hungry Caterpillar*, Puffin

Hedderwick, M., *Katie Morag and the Two Grandmothers*, Armada

Hughes, S., *Alfie Gets in First*, Armada

Hutchins, P., *Don't Forget the Bacon*, Picture Puffin

Hutchins, P., *Rosie's Walk*, Bodley Head/Puffin

Kerr, J., *Mog in the Dark*, Armada

Lord, J. V., *The Giant Jam Sandwich*, Pan Books

Nicoll, H. and Pienkowski, J., *Meg and Mog*, Picture Puffin

Nicoll, H. and Pienkowski, J., *Owl at School*, Picture Puffin

Sutton, E., *My Cat Likes to Hide in Boxes*, Picture Puffin

Tolstoy, A. and Oxenbury, H., *The Great Big Enormous Turnip*, Armada

Vipont, E. and Briggs, R., *The Elephant and the Bad Baby*, Picture Puffin

Counting books

Adams, P., *There were Ten in the Bed*, Childs Play

Bradman, T., *The Bad Babies Counting Book*, Piccadilly/Beaver

Gretz, S., *Teddy Bears 1 to 10*, Collins

Peppe, R., *Circus Numbers*, Viking Kestrel

Books for teachers

Finally, we should like to recommend these books for teachers:

Clemson, D. and Clemson, W. (1994) *Mathematics in the Early Years*, Routledge

Deboys, M. and Pitt, E. (1980) *Lines of Development in Primary Mathematics* (2nd ed.), Blackstaff Press

Hughes, M. (1986) *Children and Number*, Basil Blackwell

Merttens, R. (1987) *Teaching Primary Maths*, Edward Arnold

Williams, E. and Shuard, H. (1982) *Primary Mathematics Today* (3rd ed.), Longman

Also the Association of Teachers of Mathematics and the Mathematical Association produce a wide range of booklets and other resources.

LINKS WITH OTHER BOOKS IN THE BLUEPRINTS SERIES

You will find that the maths work in this book can be supported by activities and copymasters in other **Blueprints** books. The index below references related books which you have or may wish to acquire. References are given by copymaster number. All references refer to the 1995 editions of books. References are made to the areas of the programme of study and their numerical subdivisions.

Number

2. Developing an understanding of place value
Maths Investigations: Copymasters i, iii, iv, 3, 9, 17, School maths day (whole school investigations); **History Key Stage 1:** Counting and measuring topic.

3. Understanding relationships between numbers
Maths Investigations: Copymasters viii, 4, 6, 24; **History Key Stage 1:** Money and shops topic, Counting and measuring topic.

4. Solving numerical problems
Maths Investigations: all the activities involve problem-solving strategies, for example v and vi; **History Key Stage 1:** Money and shops topic.

5. Classifying, representing and interpreting data
Maths Investigations: Copymasters vii, 2, 10, 18, Data day (whole school investigations); **History Key Stage 1:** all topics; **Science Investigations:** Copymasters 2, 6, 8.

Shape, space and measures

2. Understanding and using patterns and properties of shapes
Maths Investigations: Copymaster 1; **History Key Stage 1:** Counting and measuring topic.

COVERAGE OF THE CURRICULUM FOR SCOTLAND, WALES AND NORTHERN IRELAND

Blueprints Maths Key Stage 1 covers nearly all the different maths curriculum requirements in place for 5–7 year olds in Wales, Scotland and Northern Ireland.

We have set out below the key curriculum content for the relevant stages for Scotland and Northern Ireland.

SCOTTISH NATIONAL GUIDELINES FOR MATHS 5–14 ▷

We have correlated the activities in this book against the attainment targets for Information Handling, Number, Money and Measurement, and Shape, Position and Movement Levels A–C. References are made to the numbered areas of study in this book for Number (pages 6–72, marked N) and Shape, Space and Measurement (pages 73–108, marked SSM).

INFORMATION HANDLING ATTAINMENT TARGET ▷

Level A	Level B	Level C
Collect		
Obtain information from a picture, video, or story N47	Obtain information from pictures, diagrams N54	Obtaining information from a variety of sources N57
Collect information about selves N47	Conduct a class survey N54	Conduct a survey beyond the class
Organise		
Tallying	Use a tally sheet N49	Using a grouped tally sheet
Counting N47	Use a simple database N53	Entering data in a table
Sorting into specific sets N45		Using a database N54
Display		
Using real objects N45, 47	Using labels, charts or diagrams N48, 51	Constructing table or chart N56
Using pictures N45–47	Constructing a bar graph, graduated in units N50, 55	Constructing a bar graph, graduated in multiple units
Drawing simple diagrams N45, 46, 48, 51		
Interpret		
From displays, locating and counting N47–49	From displays asking specific questions N49, 50	From displays and databases N52, 54

NUMBER, MONEY AND MEASUREMENT ATTAINMENT TARGET

Level A	Level B	Level C
Range and type of numbers		
Whole numbers 0–20 N1–6, 12, 33, 34 Halves N10	Whole numbers to 100 then 1000 N7, 8 Quarters N10	Whole numbers to 10,000 N8 Thirds, fifths, eighths, tenths, and simple equivalents Decimals to two places N11, 33
Money		
1p, 2p, 5p, 10p, 20p coins N34, 39	Coins up to £1 N11, 35, 39, 41	Coins/notes to £5 N11, 41
Add and subtract		
Mentally 0–10 N21–25, 34, 35 Money applications to 10p	Mentally 0–20 N12, 26 2 digits – without calculator N32 2 digits added to or subtracted from 3 digits – with calculator N33 Money applications to £1 N11, 35	Mentally one digit to or from numbers up to 3 digits N44 Subtraction by 'adding on' N32, 38 Without calculator – whole numbers with 2 digits added to or subtracted from 3 digits N42 With calculator for 3 digit whole numbers Money applications to £20 N11
Multiply and divide		
	Mentally 2, 3, 4, 5, 10 N27–31 Without calculator 2 digit numbers by 2, 3, 4, 5, 10 With calculator for 2 digit numbers multiplied/divided by any digits Applications to £1	Mentally all tables to 10 N44 Mentally 2 or 3 digits by 10 N32, 38 Without calculator 2 digits by 1 digit N48 With calculator 2 or 3 digits by 1 or 2 digits N32, 38 Applications to £20 N11
Round numbers		
	Round 2 digit whole numbers to nearest 10 N9, 43, 44	Round 3 digit whole numbers to nearest 10

Level A	Level B	Level C
Fractions, percentages and ratios		
	Find halves and quarters N10	Find simple fractions
Patterns and sequences		
Simple number sequences	Even and odd numbers N3	Patterns within tables N19, 20
Copy, continue simple patterns	Whole number sequences N18	
	More complex sequences N14	
Functions and equations		
	Find missing numbers N36, 37	Use simple function machines N37, 40
Measure and estimate		
Non-standard units: length etc. SSM19	Length SSM21, 22	Weight beyond 20 kg SSM22
Place pairs of objects in order SSM16, 17	Weight	Volume SSM22
Estimate length SSM19	Order objects in length and weight	Area
Use and understand vocabulary SSM16, 17	Use abbreviations SSM22	Estimate length and weight SSM23
	Length conservation	Select appropriate measuring devices and units SSM25
	Read scales SSM22	Read scales SSM25
		Weight and area conservation
Time		
Events in time sequence SSM18, N13	Events in time sequence	Use 12 hour timetables
Time activities in non-standard units SSM18	Tell time using analogue displays SSM22	Conventions for recording time
Tell time in whole hours SSM22	Read time using digital displays SSM22	Work with hours, minutes
		Use calendars

SHAPE, POSITION AND MOVEMENT ATTAINMENT TARGET

Level A	Level B	Level C
Range of shapes		
Classify shapes SSM1	Respond to written/oral descriptions of shapes SSM4, 6	Identify 2D shapes within 3D SSM7
Identify and name cubes, cones, cylinders and spheres SSM1, 2, 5	Identify and name triangular/square pyramid SSM2	Draw circles
Identify and name squares, triangles and circles SSM1, 3	Find shapes that will tile SSM3	Recognise 3D shapes from 2D drawings SSM5
Create or copy 3D structures SSM2	Make 3D shapes SSM2	
Position and movement		
Position and movement of object SSM9, 10	Give and understand instructions for turning through right angles SSM12	Describe features of a journey or route
Locate an object in the classroom N14, SSM11	Recognise and name the four compass points	Create paths on squared paper SSM15
	Use grid references	
	Create a square or rectangle SSM13	
Symmetry		
	Recognise symmetrical shapes SSM8	Find lines of symmetry
		Complete a symmetrical shape
Angles		
	Draw right angle SSM12	Know that a right angle = 90°
		Use 'right, acute, obtuse' to describe angles
		Know that a straight line = 180°

THE NATIONAL CURRICULUM FOR NORTHERN IRELAND FOR KEY STAGE 1

Because the programme of study for the National Curriculum for Northern Ireland is under review at the time of going to press, we have correlated the activities in this book against the Key Stage 1 statements of attainment for the maths content attainment targets (Number, Algebra, Shape and Space, Measures and Data Handling) as set out in the 1990 document. This book is correlated against Levels 1–3 of that document by level and lettered statement of attainment. Numbers refer to areas of study in this book.

Attainment Target N: Number

All the activities in this AT are contained within the programme of study for Number on pages 6–72 of this book.

Level 1
a: 1–6, 34, 35;　**b:** 1, 2;　**c:** 12;　**d:** 21–25, 36;
e: 45, 46;　**f:** 10

Level 2
a: 7, 18–20;　**b:** 10;　**c:** 44;　**d:** 11, 41;　**e:** 9

Level 3
a: 7, 8;　**b:** 10;　**c:** 10–11;　**d:** 26, 44;　**e:** 11, 41;
f: 27–31;　**g:** 27–33;　**h:** 9, 43–44

Attainment Target A: Algebra

All the activities in this AT are contained within the programme of study for Number on pages 6–72 of this book.

Level 1
13, 14

Level 2
a: 14–16;　**b:** 17, 38;　**c:** 32;　**d:** 3, 39;　**e:** 36

Level 3
a: 26;　**b:** —;　**c:** 31;　**d:** 37, 40

Attainment Target M: Measures

All the activities in this AT are contained within the programme of study for Shape, Space and Measures on pages 73–108 of this book.

Level 1
6–18

Level 2
a: 19–20;　**b:** 11, 35, 41;　**c:** 21–22

Level 3
a: 21–22;　**b:** 47;　**c:** 48

Attainment Target S: Shape and Space

All the activities in this AT are contained within the programme of study for Shape, Space and Measures on pages 73–108 of this book.

Level 1
a: 1, 2, 3, 4, 5;　**b:** 4, 5, 6, 7;　**c:** 9;　**d:** 9

Level 2
a: 4–7;　**b:** 10, 11, 14;　**c:** 12, 13, 15　**d:** 11, 14

Level 3
a: 12;　**b:** 13;　**c:** 8

Attainment Target D: Handling Data

All the activities in this AT are contained within the programme of study for Number on pages 6–72 of this book.

Level 1
a: 45, 46;　**b:** 47;　**c:** 48

Level 2
a: 46;　**b:** 49;　**c:** 50;　**d:** 51;　**e:** —　**f:** —

Level 3
a: —;　**b:** 53, 54;　**c:** 56;　**d:** 52, 57;　**e:** —;　**f:** —

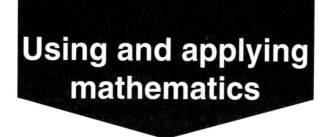

Using and applying mathematics

Key Stage 1 Programme of Study

The sections of the programme of study interrelate. Developing mathematical language, selecting and using materials, and developing reasoning, should be set in the context of the other areas of mathematics. Sorting, classifying, making comparisons and searching for patterns should apply to work on number, shape and space, and handling data. The use of number should permeate work on measures and handling data.

'Using and applying mathematics' 'threads through' 'Number' and 'Shape, space and measures'. We are confident that if the children with whom you are working have experience of a wide variety of the activities in this book, they will embrace the demands of 'Using and applying mathematics'. To illustrate this we have included below, under the relevant points in the Programme of Study, examples of activities drawn from the body of the book which meet these requirements.

Using and applying mathematics

■ 1. Pupils should be given opportunities to:

a use and apply mathematics in practical tasks, in real-life problems and within mathematics itself;

> Number: Area of study 9
>
> Shape, space and measures: Area of study 17

b explain their thinking to support the development of their reasoning.

> Number: Area of study 10
>
> Shape, space and measures: Area of study 46

■ 2. Making and monitoring decisions to solve problems

Pupils should be taught to

a select and use the appropriate mathematics;

> Number: Area of study 42
>
> Shape, space and measures: Area of study 25

b select and use mathematical equipment and materials;

> Number: Area of study 5
>
> Shape, space and measures: Area of study 25

c develop different mathematical approaches and look for ways to overcome difficulties;

> Number: Area of study 38
>
> Shape, space and measures: Area of study 13

d organise and check their work.

> Number: Area of study 43
>
> Shape, space and measures: Area of study 57

■ 3. Developing mathematical language and communication

a understand the language of number, properties of shapes and comparatives, *eg 'bigger than'*, *'next to'*, *'before'*;

> Number: Area of study 6
>
> Shape, space and measures: Area of study 17

b relate numerals and other mathematical symbols, *eg* '+', '=', to a range of situations;

> Number: Area of study 26

c discuss their work, responding to and asking mathematical questions;

> Number: Area of study 29
>
> Shape, space and measures: Area of study 45

d use a variety of forms of mathematical presentation.

> Number: Area of study 26

■ 4. Developing mathematical reasoning

a recognise simple patterns and relationships and make related predictions about them;

| Number: Area of study 16 |

b ask questions including 'What would happen if?' and 'Why?', *eg considering the behaviour of a programmable toy*;

| Shape, space and measures: Area of study 6 |

c understand general statements, *eg 'all even numbers divide by 2'*, and investigate whether particular cases match them.

| Number: Area of study 20 |

Attainment target 1: Using and applying mathematics

Level 1

Pupils use mathematics as an integral part of classroom activities. They represent their work with objects or pictures and discuss it. They recognise and use a simple pattern or relationship, usually based on their experience.

Level 2

Pupils select the mathematics for some classroom activities. They discuss their work using familiar mathematical language and are beginning to represent it using symbols and simple diagrams. They ask and respond appropriately to questions including 'What would happen if...?.

Level 3

Pupils try different approaches and find ways of overcoming difficulties that arise when they are solving problems. They are beginning to organise their work and check results. Pupils discuss their mathematical work and are beginning to explain their thinking. They use and interpret mathematical symbols and diagrams. Pupils show that they understand a general statement by finding particular examples that match it.

Number

Number

Number is one of the two major building blocks of mathematics, the other being *shape and space*. Without a sense of number and an appreciation of the power of number, children cannot make progress into areas of mathematics such as *algebra* and *data handling*.

In one sense it could be argued that number has been, and continues to be, the major pre-occupation of primary school mathematics for it partly matches the old arithmetic of the 'three R's'. Even a cursory glance into many primary schools would provide ample evidence that children's mathematical experience can be directly linked to the doing of sums.

What the National Curriculum offers, though, is a much broader definition of mathematics than pages of sums, for the requirements in relation to number work are themselves much broader than what has been traditionally offered. In order to grapple with number work in the context of the National Curriculum, children and teachers have to embrace a wide range of activities, many of them not amenable to pencil-and-paper operations. For example, where exploration and appreciation of number patterns may once have been seen by some as recreational mathematics (not proper maths!) it is now seen as an essential part of the ways children can come to understand number. The aim is to enable children to manipulate and use number. In this section of the book we offer a range of practical activities and, where appropriate, paper-and-pencil opportunities through which children can start on the road to using numbers for their own purposes – and to do so with a sense of enjoyment and achievement.

Resourcing number

In addition to a selection of the resources we have listed at the beginning of this book, the following will prove useful in carrying through some of the activities in this section:

- A play house with tea-set, dolls, a play table and chairs, pans and a play cooker, purses, handbags, hats, paper flowers
- Play food, including some made in two halves
- A telephone book, pretend parcels
- Plastic money and play paper notes
- A freezer thermometer and a maximum and minimum thermometer.

Algebra

For some people, *algebra* conjures up experiences of learning tricks that can be done with numbers and letters, but to no obvious purpose. It is an area of mathematics that provokes strong feelings. This is a pity because the purpose of algebra is to simplify understanding through the generation of generalisations about such things as number patterns or the path of a line on a graph. In tackling early work in algebra, we need to keep in mind the idea about generalising from the particular. For children to make sense of the purpose of algebra, they need the opportunity to work with lots of numbers before they can see a generalisable pattern.

There are two main ways in which the foundations of some aspects of algebra are found in primary classrooms. Children often encounter 'sums' which invite them to state what is the missing number. These are often of the form $4 + ? = 6$. While there are connections with algebraic ideas it must not be assumed that algebra is only about handling equations (although that is a skill within algebra), but rather that equations are formulations of general statements derived from sets of real data. It is important to understand what equations and formulae actually represent. The other encounter with algebra many children have is when teachers ask for a general statement of the kind: 'What sort of a number (or sequence of numbers) is that?'

The foundations of algebra, as set out in the National Curriculum, pay attention in the early years to relationships and sequences as well as patterns and the generation of generalisations.

Resourcing algebra

The resource bank that we mention at the front of the book is appropriate for work in this section. Additional resources that may help include:

- A tape or record of sound patterns like birdsong and roadworks
- A camera and film
- Musical instruments
- Poetry books
- Feely bags
- An ark and animals
- A Celsius thermometer scale.

You may wish to pursue pattern-making ideas in art and technology. These will demand a variety of materials and media, including all those mentioned in the general resource bank.

Good use can be made of the newer technologies. Computers, good software and, if possible, 'robot' devices will reap rewards in both understanding and motivation.

Handling data

It is on the basis of data that we manage our lives. Much of our decision-making is based upon the assembling of data, its interpretation and the prediction of likely events based upon that interpretation. The exent to which we make decisions that are reasoned and reasonable has much to do with the quality, scope and analysis of data. On the other hand, we can leave it all to fate! From these statements you will gather that we see data handling as being an important area of application in mathematics.

As in science there is a need to organise the format and scope of any data collection activity and then have the persistence to carry through that data collection – and to do so without starting to interpret what is being collected too soon. Leaping to conclusions on the basis of partial data is not acceptable and this is one of the often difficult things that we need to draw out of our data handling work. Additionally, of course, it is important to help the children to see that different sources of data may need tapping in different ways and this is also part of a planned data collection activity. The form in which data comes will affect the ways in which it can be analysed and interpreted.

Presenting data in an understandable and clear form is the final piece of the jigsaw, since constructing meaningful pictorial representations needs the author of the work to have understood that data. It is also the case that the choice of representation must be sensibly linked to the type of data and its organisation.

So data handling is a complex activity characterised by the need to plan, the need to be patient and persistent, and the need to have a wide repertoire of techniques and methods of presentation at your fingertips. The early work in data handling sets out to establish important foundations in all of these areas.

Resourcing this section

You need data! You can get it at second hand, by looking for lists, tables, frequency charts and block graphs already available. Though these are important they do not replace the first-hand data that the children as researchers collect in school. It may also be useful to have a cardboard grid similar to dividers in wine boxes to start the children off in making concrete block graphs.

Attainment target 2: Number and algebra

Level descriptions

Level 1

Pupils count, order, add and subtract numbers when solving problems involving up to 10 objects. They read and write the numbers involved. Pupils recognise and make repeating patterns, counting the number of each object in each repeat.

Level 2

Pupils count sets of objects reliably, and use mental recall of addition and subtraction facts to 10. They have begun to understand the place value of each digit in a number and use this to order numbers up to 100. They choose the appropriate operation when solving addition and subtraction problems. They identify and use halves and quarters, such as half of a rectangle or a quarter of eight objects. They recognise sequences of numbers, including odd and even numbers.

Level 3

Pupils show understanding of place value in numbers up to 1000 and use this to make approximations. They have begun to use decimal notation and to recognise negative numbers, in contexts such as money, temperature and calculator displays. Pupils use mental recall of addition and subtraction facts to 20 in solving problems involving larger numbers. They use mental recall of the 2, 5 and 10 multiplication tables, and others up to 5 × 5, in solving whole-number problems involving multiplication or division, including those that give rise to remainders. Pupils use calculator methods where numbers include several digits. They have begun to develop mental strategies, and use them to find methods for adding and subtracting numbers with at least two digits.

Programme of study: Number

■ 1. Pupils should be given opportunities to:

a develop flexible methods of working with number, orally and mentally;

b encounter numbers greater than 1000;

c use a variety of practical resources and contexts;

d use calculators both as a means to explore number and as a tool for calculating with realistic data, *eg numbers with several digits*;

e record in a variety of ways, including ways that relate to their mental work;

f use computer software, including a database.

For this part of the Programme of Study we have set down examples drawn from the body of the book which will meet these points.

a Area of study 21

b Area of study 8

c Area of study 14

d Area of study 33

e Area of study 44

f Area of study 54

Number

How the Areas of study in this book fit the Programme of study and Attainment target 2: Number and Algebra level descriptions.

Points in the Programme of study	Areas of study and 'best fit' with level descriptions		
	Level description 1	Level description 2	Level description 3
2. Developing an understanding of place value			
a count orally up to 10 and beyond, knowing the number names; count collections of objects, checking the total; count in steps of different sizes, *eg count on from 5 in steps of 2 or 3*; recognise sequences, including odd and even numbers;	1, 2	3	
b read, write and order numbers, initially to 10, progressing up to 1000, developing an understanding that the position of a digit signifies its value; begin to approximate larger numbers to the nearest 10 or 100;	4, 5, 6	7	8, 9
c recognise and use in context simple fractions, including halves and quarters, decimal notation in recording money, and negative numbers, *eg a temperature scale, a number line, a calculator display.*		10	11, 12
3 Understanding relationships between numbers and developing methods of computation			
a use repeating patterns to develop ideas of regularity and sequencing;	13, 14, 15		
b explore and record patterns in addition and subtraction, and then patterns of multiples, *eg 3, 6, 9, 12*, explaining their patterns and using them to make predictions; progress to exploring further patterns involving multiplication and division, including those within a hundred-square of multiplication facts;	16	17, 18	19, 20
c know addition and subtraction facts to 20, and develop a range of mental methods for finding, from known facts, those that they cannot recall; learn multiplication and division facts relating to the 2s, 5s, 10s, and use these to learn other facts, *eg double multiples of 2 to produce multiples of 4*, and to develop mental methods for finding new results;	21, 22, 23, 24	25, 26	27, 28, 29, 30, 31
d develop a variety of methods for adding and subtracting, including using the fact that subtraction is the inverse of addition; • use a basic calculator, reading the display, *eg use the constant function to explore repeated addition.*		33	32

7

Number

How the Areas of study in this book fit the Programme of study and Attainment target 2: Number and Algebra level descriptions.

Areas of study and 'best fit' with level descriptions

Points in the Programme of study	Level description 1	Level description 2	Level description 3
4. Solving numerical problems			
a understand the operations of addition, subtraction as taking away and comparison, and the relationship between them, recognise situations to which they apply and use them to solve problems with whole numbers, including situations involving money;	34	35, 36, 37, 38, 39	40, 41
b understand the operations of multiplication, and division as sharing and repeated subtraction, and use them to solve problems with whole numbers or money, understanding and dealing appropriately with remainders;			40, 41
c choose a suitable method of computation, using apparatus where appropriate, or a calculator where the numbers include several digits;		39	41, 42
d begin to check answers in different ways, *eg repeating the calculation in a different order or using a different method,* and gain a feel for the appropriate size of an answer.			43, 44
5 Classifying, representing and interpreting data			
a sort and classify a set of objects using criteria related to their properties, *eg size, shape, mass;*	45, 46	Level descriptions do not apply to 5a and b	
b collect, record and interpret data arising from an area of interest, using an increasing range of charts, diagrams, tables and graphs.	47, 48, 49, 50, 51, 52, 53, 54, 55, 56		

Programme of study: Number

Pupils should be taught to:

■ **2. Developing an understanding of place value**

a count orally up to 10 and beyond, knowing the number names; count collections of objects, checking the total; count in steps of different sizes, *eg count on from 5 in steps of 2 or 3*; recognise sequences, including odd and even numbers;

Area of study 1	P of S 2a	LD 1	

BEGINNING COUNTING

Commentary

The emphasis should be on counting things that the children can see, point to, touch and handle. Work with the children in small groups so that they can all touch the items being counted, if they wish.

Encourage the children to count from left to right along a row of items. As far as possible, always present the items for counting like this during the work at Level 1.

The children need plenty of practice in counting real things. Most of the mathematics used in everyday life is based on this; through their own practical experiences, children will come to understand that counting and maths are about real life, and are important and useful.

Much maths is about comparisons, so help the children to compare numbers and find ways of connecting them.

Do not introduce numerals or ask children to record too soon. Recording the result of a count is a separate operation, and not part of the count. Numerals form a new language for children. The children should, for example, have an understanding of what 'two' of many different things look and feel like – and where they might find 'twos' – before they are introduced to the squiggle '2' used as a sign for 'two'.

Activity 1: The children themselves

Get a small group of children to sit close to you, facing you. Ask a child to stand in front of the group, and while you point, let the children count aloud with you. Point to his/her legs, ears, pigtails, buttons, shoes, fingers and any other features that can be counted, like badges or stripes. Restrict your choices to numbers lower than ten. As far as possible, point and count from left to right *from the children's point of view.*

When the children have seen you point and count, and have counted along with you many times, they can each have turns at pointing and counting. Their practice in counting from left to right with you should transfer to their own counting.

When the children are familiar with group counting, ask more children to stand in front of the group to enable counting of 'sorts'. For example, the children can count the number of boys, girls, people with blue eyes, big toes, cardigans, etc.

They can look at and compare numbers of things; for example, you can ask all the children with cardigans to stand in a separate row from those without.

Activity 2: Counting everyday objects

Assemble collections of like objects with ten in each. Conkers and pencils, crayons and rulers, books and blocks are fine, but do make sure your collections include things of varying sizes, materials and colours, and containers with a range of different contents, so that the children understand that all these factors are irrelevant in counting. You could have a variety of different sized cereal packets; a collection of socks, including ones for a baby and an adult's walking or football sock; a set of hats, including a rain hat, felt hat, paper party hat and a doll's hat. Add a dolls' house chair to a row of classroom chairs, a paperhanging brush to your collection of paintbrushes; include full and empty jam-jars in a collection, and several varieties in a collection of nuts.

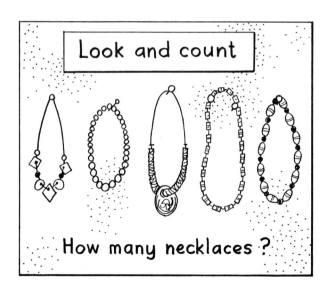

Look and count

How many necklaces?

Ask the children to count across kinds of things. Make a display where on Monday there are vases to count, on Tuesday beads, on Wednesday books, and on Thursday and Friday a miscellany. Vary the display to make it novel and inviting, but always make sure the things for counting lie from left to right.

Monday's counting

Friday's counting

Count the boxes

How many teddies are having a balloon ride?

Activity 3: Counting lines, rows and clusters or groups
Once the children have a good grasp of counting from left to right, you can introduce counting a column and a cluster. Use a display board to mount things that children can count upwards and downwards. These could be soft toys, matchboxes – in fact, any items that you can attach to a backing board.

Teachers' handbags

teacher's drawings

Simon's drinks

cut-outs from magazines

Adele's suns

child's drawings

Susie's shells

magazine pictures

Pat's grandads

photos

Count the pictures

Look for naturally occurring clusters like the number of leaves on a twig, or birds on the bird-table. Point out everyday groups of things for counting, for example, fruit in a bowl, a handful of crayons, the flowers in a vase. Show the children patterns in which groups often appear, like the dots on a die. (See also the activities under Area of study 2 'Conservation games'.)

Activity 4: One-to-one correspondence

Using the home-corner tea-set, the dolls' house tea-set or some crockery and cutlery borrowed from the kitchen, let the children practise setting table for their friends, or the dolls. Ask them to give each doll a plate, bowl, and so on.

The children could devise their own games like giving each friend a crayon, a badge, a skipping rope, a drink, or a letter to take home.

Activity 5: Counting at secondhand

From a small group of children, through discussion, gather counting information about themselves, including, for example, how many

people live in their house

pets they have (beware the 57 goldfish!)
sisters they have
Shredded Wheat® they eat
pairs of shoes they have
five-year-olds there are.

Collect pictures of kinds of things from magazines, catalogues and advertisements. Mount them and store them in transparent folders or large envelopes. The children can lay these out to count. You can also ask them to search for, cut out and count collections of their own. Display your pictures and theirs in a 'counting corner'. Note that the children are not using numerals yet.

Activity 6: Counting rhymes

To reinforce the pattern of words used in number, teach the children some rhymes; for example, 'One, two, three, four, five, once I caught a fish alive', 'This old man', 'One, two, buckle my shoe', 'One finger, one thumb, keep moving'. Make up some with the children. For example, 'One, two, listen and do; three, four, sit on the floor; Kevin, please will you shut the door?' will have much appeal for Kevin and his friends.

Area of study 2	P of S 2a	LD 1	**CONSERVATION GAMES**	C1-6, R1

Commentary

You will be able to observe whether individual children are beginning to conserve number, when they add to a count they have started and are confident about counting on, without going back to the beginning.

To conserve, they should recognise that a counted set is the same, no matter how the individual objects are arranged.

Number games can be played at all stages in children's mathematical development. We have put dice games under 'Conservation' because a die can present a pattern of 'three', for example, in a number of ways. Here are some:

Dice with dots on them can be used to test conservation, while numeral dice help consolidate number recognition. Some toy shops sell loose dice with varying numbers of sides, enabling children to show their understanding of conservation beyond six.

Activity 1: Let's conserve

In a group, give each child a toy, or marble or brick, letting the children count as you go. Ask how many there are altogether. Then distribute the same items unevenly around the group, omitting some children and giving others several items. Ask how many altogether. Vary this again and again until all the children are convinced that the number of objects is always the same. Play with a set of Unifix® or oranges or something else to count, moving them about to make different patterns, and quiz the children each time about how many there are altogether. They can record their observations, construct their own patterns of a number and record them.

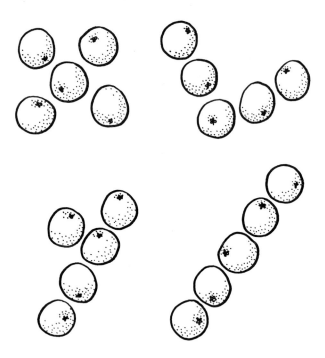

Copymaster 1 (Conservation of 5) gives the children a chance to record some work on number patterns.

Copymaster 2 (Conservation of 2, 3, 5) depicts dominoes. Encourage the children to look at the patterns on whole dominoes as well as those on each half.

Activity 2: Dice games
Let the children play track games on boards without numbers, to consolidate their recognition and conservation of number to 10. Start with a blank die, or cardboard spinner, on which you write configurations of two and three dots. **Resource copymaster R1** (Spinners) may be useful here.

The game on **copymaster 3** (Ladybird race) can be played with a die or spinner.

The games on **copymaster 4** (Cheese chase) and **5** (Home-time!) can be played with a die with any pattern of numbers on them. **Copymaster 6** (Aliens) is a die/numeral recognition game to 6 for two players; the players throw the die in turn, colouring a section of the alien that matches the die score.

Activity 3: Card games
A conventional pack of cards has number sequences to 10 in each suit, but the numbers are inverted at the bottom of each card. Instead, make your own pack using dots rather than numerals. You could have as many suits (by colour or shape of dots) as you like.

The children could play a memory game with the cards. Shuffle the cards and spread out face down. Let each child turn up two cards to try for a matching pair.

The children could also play 'Snap'.

Area of study 3	P of S 2a	LD 2		C7, 8

ODDS AND EVENS

Commentary
Mathematicians use a variety of means to sort numbers out, using ideas such as prime, square, cube, triangular and hexagonal numbers and so on. Odds and evens is one way which has been adopted in everyday life.

We feel that children should understand place value before trying to master odds and evens beyond 10. To say that 36 is an even number really means that you should not only know it is because the last digit is a 6 and that is divisible by 2, but that the whole number can be divided by 2.

Activity 1: Explaining odds and evens
Put out a small number of objects (for example, seven marbles) in front of a group of children. Ask: 'How many marbles are there? Can we put them into twos? Yes, there are three twos but there is an odd one left over. We say seven is an odd number.' Try again with, for example, four pencils. Tell the children that four is called an even number.

Invent a diagrammatic way to represent odds and evens. For example, you could draw a staircase with

even numbers on the treads and odds on the risers, or they can be placed on a zigzag with odds at the bottom and evens at the top.

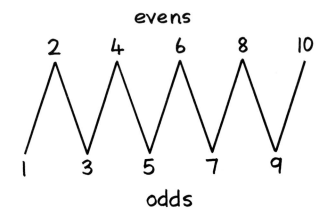

Copymaster 7 (Odds and evens) presents the children with a sorting activity for odd and even numbers to 10.

Activity 2: Oral odds and evens

As soon as you have introduced the concept of odd and even, the children can respond to oral work on these. They can play 'LOUD ODDS, quiet evens' while counting aloud to 20. They can sing the odds and 'growl' the evens! Ask a child to walk across the classroom. Note which is her or his leading foot, and then pin a label saying 'odd' to this foot. Attach an 'even' label to the other foot. Now ask her or him to walk across again while the children count aloud; the child's steps should match the odd and even labels.

Count aloud again and again, letting the children do a whole series of actions to rehearse the pattern of odds and evens; for example, putting their hands up for the odd numbers and/or putting their finger on their chin for even numbers. Let them have turns with a shaker or drum to make a sound when they hear an odd number.

Activity 3: Practice with odds and evens

Give the children some practical sorting activities, using odd and even numbers. For example, stick numbers onto cardboard houses, attach age badges to the toys and number some pictures of raffle prizes.

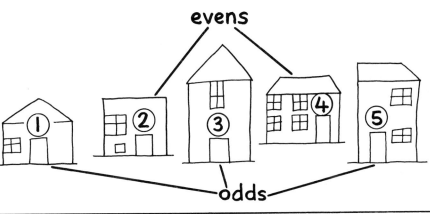

evens

odds

How old are the toys?

Who is an <u>odd</u> number of years old?

If these were raffle prizes which would you like to win? Does it have an odd or even number?

13

Copymaster 8 (Prize-winning numbers) lets the children identify odd and even numbers where the odds win a prize.

Activity 4: Numbers we know
Make a book of all the numbers that are important to the children, identifying which are odd and even. Each child may like to fill a page to add to a number book for all the class to look at.

Programme of study: Number

Pupils should be taught to:

■ **2. Developing an understanding of place value**   **b** read, write and order numbers, initially to 10, progressing up to 1000, developing an understanding that the position of a digit signifies its value; begin to approximate larger numbers to the nearest 10 or 100;

Area of study	P of S	LD		C9
4	2b	1	**NOTATION AND RECORDING THE SIZE OF COUNTS**	-13

Commentary

When children start recording numbers, both they and their parents may feel that real mathematics is just beginning. This is probably because in the past computational skills have been seen as the most important part of maths. However, it is important to combat the pressures of the 'pages of sums' approach and continue to let the children work practically as much as possible. They could probably master all they need to know about the numbers one to ten without writing down anything, but reading and writing soon start to affect progress in number work. Practice in reading and writing, including that done during maths sessions, is important.

The first step is to give the children the idea that recording the number of a count can help us to remember it, so that we can replicate it or use it for further work. For example, we write down how many pints of milk are on order, so that we know what to order next week if we find we had too much or too little (assisting memory), and so that we can check our milk bill (further work, in this case computation).

We have included one activity on 'pairs'. Because so much about us is paired, the concept is used frequently. This is an example of a word in common use having a relationship with mathematical ideas.

Activity 1: Numerals attached to counts

When the children are competent at counting aloud, having had plenty of practice, introduce the numerals.

Here are several activities to do on a 'one' day. Follow up with reinforcement/consolidation activities and then repeat some of the tasks for 'two', 'three', 'four', and so on. Ask the children to:

● Draw themselves, one balloon, one lollipop, one cake, and so on
● Put out a range of containers and put one item in each
● Mount and display a range of pictures each with a single item in them.

Now you have a variety of 'ones' to attach a numeral to. First, draw a number '1' on the board, on a piece of paper with a paintbrush or in the sandtray, making sure that all the children are in a position to see that a '1' is drawn as a vertical line, starting at the top.

Get the children to pretend they each have a 'magic' finger and draw 1s in the air. Now let the children go round the pictures and draw magic 1s on each. Then, letting them work individually, give them a supply of little labels each with the numeral 1 on them. They can attach the numerals to things around the classroom. This is their first record of a counting exercise.

Activity 2: Numerals in sequence

Arrange a counting table or display like those in the 'Beginning counting' activities above. Let the children have turns and watch while each does a series of counting exercises and matches the appropriate numeral.

Arrange a display which can be regularly and frequently changed over a period of weeks, to give the children opportunities to match numerals to the appropriate counts.

Activity 3: Beads in lines and rows
Ask the children to thread a number of beads on a string. They can match a numeral to each of the beads, laying the beads first horizontally and then vertically.

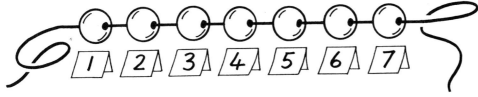

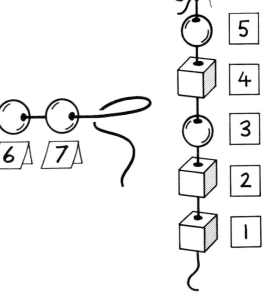

Activity 4: Putting a numeral to actual counts
Let the children write, trace, paint, draw, colour and make the shapes of the numeral which matches their actual counts. So, if they lay six shells in a sand tray, they can draw '6' in the sand. If they make a model bird with three feathers in its tail, they can do a seed trail to make a numeral '3' to attach to the tail.

Activity 5: Matching numerals to pictures
Encourage the children to record how many trees, windows, clouds, etc. there are in their own pictures and in pictures you provide.

Copymaster 9 (Numeral–set match) and 10–12 (Counting and recording counts) present some exercises in counting and matching.

Activity 6: Number lines
On cardboard strips marked off in ten equal sections, write in, or let the children write in, the numerals. Set a number of objects along the line, and say how many altogether. Let the children count groups or sets of objects and check their counts by matching them against the number line.

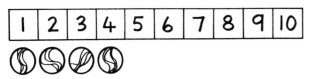

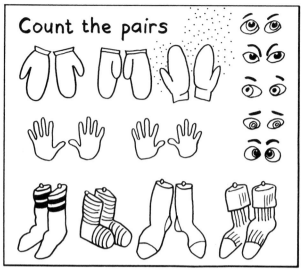

Count the pairs

Noah's Ark

Activity 7: Pairs

Two socks are not a pair unless they match. The notion of 'pair' seems to carry with it a connection beyond 'twoness'. In fact, it would seem that to talk of a pair engages with two mathematical ideas, namely the number and the membership of a set. Discuss the pairs to be seen on human beings, including pairs of eyes, ears, legs and hands, and give the children work on pairs as well as the work on the number 'two'.

Copymaster 13 (Pairs) reinforces some of this work.

Area of study 5	P of S 2b	LD 1

CARDINAL AND ORDINAL NUMBERS

C14

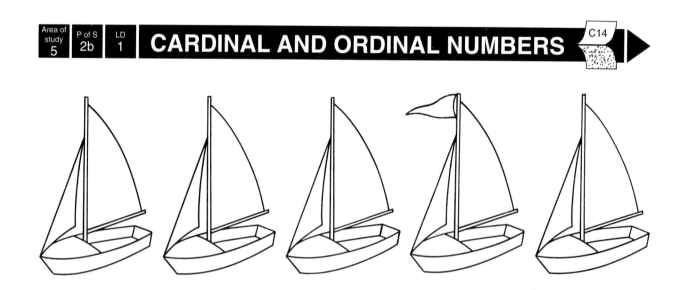

Commentary

Children need to understand that saying something is *eighth* in a row is a different use of the number 'eight' than saying that there are *eight* objects in a group. For example, when we say, 'There are five boats in the row', 'five' is a cardinal number. If we say, 'The fourth boat has a flag', we are using ordinal number. But if we were to ask for four boats, this is not asking for the fourth boat! Cardinal number gives totals and subtotals, ordinal number position. Some children find the difference between a count and a position confusing. Help them by letting them master cardinal number thoroughly first, and by not mixing cardinal and ordinal number in the same problem.

Activity 1: Ordinal number

Now that the children can count and put cardinal numbers in sequence, you can give them opportunities to put things in order. First put some objects in order, such as soft toys at a model bus stop or play food for a giant's breakfast. Then discuss who is second in the bus queue, or what is the fifth thing the giant is going to eat for breakfast. Let the children come and point to a toy or item and say its position.

Let the children create their own ordered rows, including runners or boats past a finishing line in a race, children in a line at hometime, and clothes they take off (or put on) for PE.

16

Activity 2: Ordinal number in stories and rhymes
Look for and point out ordinal numbers in stories. For example: 'The children had three wishes. What was their first wish?' 'What were the first, second and third sons given by their father?'

Activity 3: Recording ordinal number
When the children have practised naming the order of things and labelling them, they can work at recording their ordering, and complete work set out in their books on ordering.
    Copymaster 14 (Ordinal numbers) is a sample sheet of ideas.

| Area of study 6 | P of S 2b | LD 1 | | THE LANGUAGE OF NUMBER |

Commentary
While in many senses mathematics is a language in its own right, communication of mathematical ideas is usually through spoken or written language. This means that words in common use may have a special meaning in a mathematical setting, which can lead to confusion for children. We need to be constantly alert for misunderstandings of language rather than of the mathematics. Some examples of areas prone to language complications are these:

● Numbers are used in making comparisons. The vocabulary used in measurement is relevant here. We say we need *more* bottles of milk on Saturday and *more* material for a longer skirt. Children need to know that 7 is *more than* 5, but *less than* 8. Through your use of appropriate vocabulary, the children will begin to use it too.
● The existence of '0' in the number system is of vital importance, but we call it a variety of names. These include 'zero', 'nought', 'nil', and 'nothing'. Of

these, 'nothing' is probably the least helpful and is mathematically inaccurate. But whatever your choice of word, it helps to be consistent and to elaborate the meaning through regular explanations. (The children will meet '0' at Number Level 3.)
● We need to be aware of language and cultural differences. For example, in English single words identify whole numbers up to and including 20; in French word combinations are used from 17 to 19.

Activity 1: Words for numbers
Introduce children to number rhymes in books and to counting books where the number has been written as a word as well as a numeral. Make a class number book to ten, or let each child make their own.
    Put a number chart on the wall, and let the children count as a group, reading from the chart. Cover the numerals sometimes, and let them have turns at reading the number words or pointing them out to the group.

17

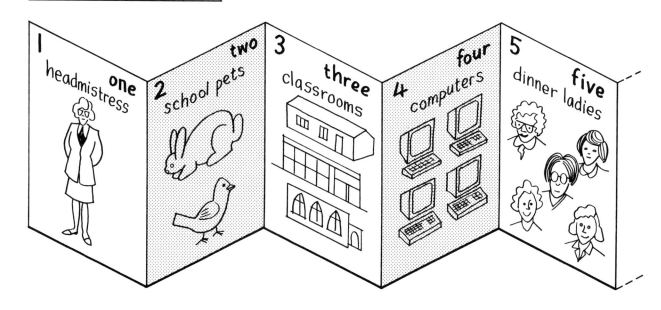

A number book

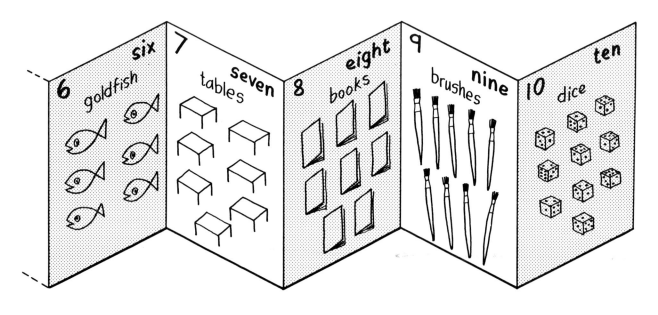

flap can be put down over numerals

1	2	3	4	5	6	7	8	9	10
one	two	three	four	five	six	seven	eight	nine	ten

flap can be put down over number words

18

Activity 2: Responding to words for numbers

Make some flash cards, each with a number word from 'one' to 'ten' on it. Use these in giving instructions. For example, in PE, hold up a card with 'two' written on it, say 'Hop' and the children have to give two hops; hold up 'six' and say 'Step' and the children have to take six steps; and so on. In music, you could give instructions to percussion players and to children clapping using number flash cards. Another possibility is to include instructions on the board or in their books which say,

for example, 'Draw two things you like to eat.' 'Find three books about dogs.'

Collect favourite numbers and information about numbers, and record number information about the children themselves on a number display or in a number book. Add some more 'abstract' numbers, including the number of days in a week, seasons in a year and so on. Use both numerals and number words, to ensure the children can use both with facility.

Activity 3: Language in maths

While the children are counting, you can begin to use words they will need in making comparisons. Here are a selection of words that can be introduced:

more than/less than
the same as
most/least
low/lower/lowest
high/higher/highest

A *Words for Numbers* book can be made for the children to consult. This should include concepts that the children have already met, such as 'pairs' and 'sets'.

Make display cards with entries like 'is more than', 'is less than'. Ask the children to practise making number sentences, using their counts and the numeral cards.

Activity 4: Matching and comparing

Let the children match two sets of items, using pieces of string or wool to join each item to its fellow in the other set. They can then say whether one set has more or less than the other.

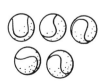 

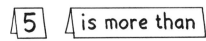
5 is more than 3

Which has more ?

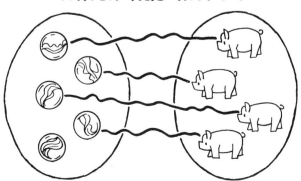

19

Area of study	P of S	LD
7	2b	2

HOW MANY TENS?

Commentary

Place value is fundamental to all number work. In order for children to manipulate numbers they must appreciate that, for example, the symbol '1' can mean a single unit, or one ten, or one hundred, or one million million!

Young children have a fascination with numbers. They often count, out loud, whole sequences of numbers – trying to get to one hundred is a common game. However, children's ability to learn the words used to describe natural numbers should not be confused with an understanding of place value. Being able to say 'twenty-three' and even write down '23' cannot be taken as evidence that the number twenty-three is understood in terms of its constitutents and the conventions used in writing it.

Activity 1: What's in a number?

The children will need a large number of counting aids for this activity. Unifix®, Multilink® or Cuisenaire® ones and tens, or spent matches and elastic bands, are ideal. The way you do this activity will depend on what aids are available.

First show the children that a number of Unifix®, say 34, can be put in a pile, or fixed end to end. Then explain that numbers are grouped so that they are easier to work with and that they are put in groups of ten. The outcome is like this:

Lay the assembled real Unifix® on a piece of card with large numerals '3' and '4' written as 34. Tell the children if nobody spots it, that there are 3 tens where the 3 is and 4 ones where the 4 is.

Try this again and again for different numbers. Then let the children lay out numbers of their own choice.

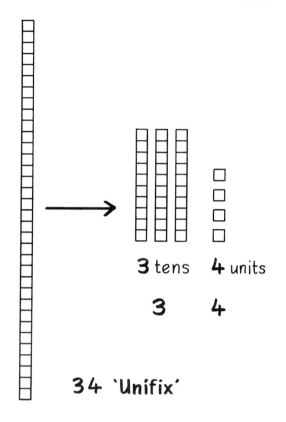

3 tens   4 units

3   4

34 'Unifix'

(Give them an upper limit or you will run out of Unifix® or Multilink®!)

Activity 2: Recording what's in a number

Let the children repeat Activity 1, and transfer their findings to their books. Drawing a tower of ten can be a problem for some children. A stencil may help.

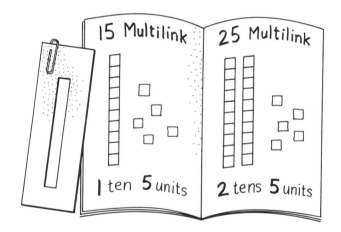

Area of study	P of S	LD
8	2b	3

NUMBERS TO 1000 AND BEYOND

C15–17
R2,3,5

Commentary

At Level 2 the children will have worked on how we write numbers, and how the placing of a digit affects what we read. Revise this, using ones and tens (Cuisenaire® or Colour Factor®) or spent matches and elastic bands to make bundles of ten. Then try some more consolidation activities.

Activity 1: Tens and units 'columns'
Show the children how to draw columns in their books for 'tens' and 'units'. Using a class chart, record some numbers up to 100 on this. Then let the children put some into their books. They can throw two dice to assemble the digits.

There is a sheet of numbers to transfer to 'tens' and 'units' columns on **copymaster 15** (Tens and units).

Activity 2: Really big numbers
Now do similar work to that in Activity 1, using numbers in the hundreds and thousands.

Copymaster 16 (Thousands, hundreds, tens and units) presents a sheet of numbers to place in 'thousands', 'hundreds', 'tens' and 'units' columns.

The children can make some 'big' numbers on a calculator to put into their books.

Activity 3: Patterns of ten
The children will, by now, be familiar with the pattern of tens up to 100. Let them count on in tens, and then make patterns with hundreds. They can fill in the numbers on a hundred square, and then lay these out to make 'hundreds' and a thousand.

Resource copymasters R2 and **R3** give hundred squares. **Resource copymaster R5** is a sheet of centimetre squares which can be used to cut out configurations of large numbers.

Activity 4: Numbers in words
When the children can tell by looking at a number whether it has 'hundreds' or 'tens' in it, give them some numbers written out as words, which they must convert to numerals.

Copymaster 17 (Big numbers in words) gives some examples that the children must translate.

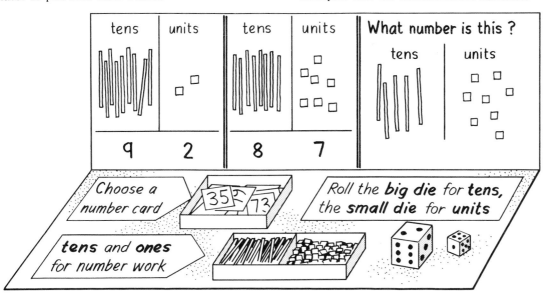

| Area of study **9** | P of S **2b** | LD **3** | ## APPROXIMATION |

Commentary
In adult life approximation is a skill we use a great deal. If there is £9.87 in our purse, we know that we have nearer ten pounds than nine. A half-full bag of flour, marked 1 kilogram, will contain approximately a pound of flour. Approximations make it easier to solve number problems. If we are buying a fence for the perimeter of the garden we know that 106.531 46 metres is not the level of accuracy needed in working out how many fencing panels to buy. Approximations and estimations are not the same; we use the former to determine the latter.

Activity 1: Give an approximation
Give the children the solutions to some problems and results of some experiments, and ask for an approximation of these.

Activity 2: Effects of approximation
Discuss with the children, the dilemmas we all face when we find something out and want to tell other people of our findings. This applies in all kinds of research situations. For example:

● Mum has discovered how many biscuits the family eats in a fortnight.
● Survey researchers have established how often Britons say they take a bath.

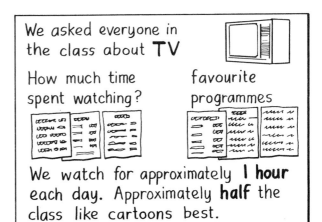

Should mum say, 'The family have eaten 96 biscuits in two weeks,' or 'Six packets of biscuits have gone in a fortnight!'? Which will make more impact on the family? Which is more accurate? Which is more useful for mum to know, if she is going to buy less in future? It may be that the approximation, that is the number of packets, is the more potent information.

So, too, would be the revelation that approximately one in ten Britons have a bath once a month!

Use some of the results the children have obtained in their research to work out approximations and their implications.

Programme of study: Number

Pupils should be taught to:

■ **2. Developing an understanding of place value**

c recognise and use in context simple fractions, including halves and quarters, decimal notation in recording money, and negative numbers, *eg a temperature scale, a number line, a calculator display.*

Area of study 10	P of S 2c	LD 2	A HALF AND A QUARTER	C18, 19

Commentary

The idea of 'halving' is probably familiar to children. They have probably all had to share a cake or a drink with another child at some time. However, it cannot be assumed that because they use 'half' and 'quarter' in everyday speech, they have a concept of what it means. Work on 'division' comes in Level 3, but you can lay the foundations for it by doing practical sharing into halves and quarters now.

Activity 1: Sharing half each

Make a number of play items, in sections so that they can be 'cut' into two, or four. For example, foam rubber sheeting makes sponge cakes, corrugated card brown

bread for sandwiches and play dough makes excellent jam tarts, sweets and other imaginary edibles. These have the advantage that they are relatively durable, and with care could last for more than one set of children.

Using two children or two toys demonstrate that sharing the sponge cake *equally* between them means that each will have a half. The sponge is the whole, and a portion is a half. Share other play edibles and encourage the children to identify each half. Give them each opportunities to have a go.

Show the children how to write the word 'half' and the '$\frac{1}{2}$' sign. (The division sign is explained in 'First divisions', Area of study 30.)

Then show the children how to share a quantity of, for example, rice or pasta.

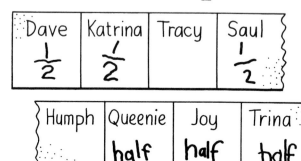

Come and write $\frac{1}{2}$ and half

Dave	Katrina	Tracy	Saul
$\frac{1}{2}$	$\frac{1}{2}$		$\frac{1}{2}$

Humph	Queenie	Joy	Trina
	half	half	half.

Activity 2: Sharing quarter each

As in Activity 1, share play items between four children or toys, and let the children have goes at doing the same.

Show the children how to write a 'quarter' and the $\frac{1}{4}$ sign. Create a wallchart with this information on it. (Draw a quarter of the shape under the flaps.)

Activity 3: Paper folding halves and quarters

With a variety of kinds of paper and a range of tasks, get the children to cut shapes into halves and quarters.

Activity 4: Recording half and quarter

Ask the children to use the play edibles to create their own ways of sharing halves and quarters and draw them in their books. Give the children additional recording that you have begun for them on worksheets or cards.

Copymaster **18** (Halves) and **19** (Quarters) give another method of presenting this work.

Make a half and quarter display, including a clock face, just showing a half and a quarter.

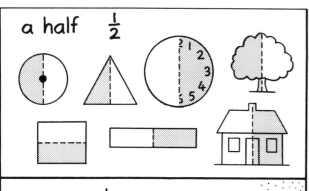

a half $\frac{1}{2}$

some puzzles
• half of your pocket money ?
• half of 10 pence ?
• half of 6 marbles ?
• halfway round the world - where is that ?

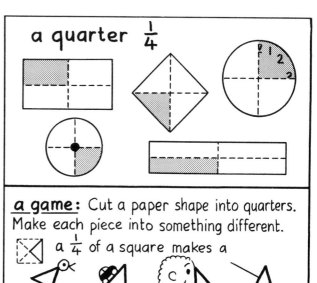

a quarter $\frac{1}{4}$

a game: Cut a paper shape into quarters. Make each piece into something different.

a $\frac{1}{4}$ of a square makes a

RECORDING MONEY

Commentary

The children will have played with replica coins at Level 2. They should have had a chance to have a close look at real coins and notes and discuss equivalence. Now is the moment to introduce the decimal point.

While the use of a decimal point is at the heart of how we record money it is important to remember that conventions in money work do not follow, in some important respects, the conventions in decimal work. For example, we do not write £1.40 as £1.4 – we always show whole numbers of pence after the decimal point.

Activity 1: Using pounds and pence

Use play coins, and print some play £5 and £10 notes. With the children, look at the values of these, match equivalent values in different coinage and discuss how we write this down on a bill. Show the children some real bills, including, for example, an electricity bill, a supermarket checkout slip and a bill from the garage or window cleaner. Use these as a basis for a display.

Tell the children about the decimal point in money, that that is what it is called, and that it marks where the number of pence begins. Make sure they understand that we have to be careful to write 08 after a decimal point, if we mean 8p, because there is a 'tens' column there.

Copymaster 20 (Tickets, bills and receipts) presents a number of bills, receipts and price layouts for discussion, and a shopping list and bill for the child to complete.

Activity 2: Writing pounds and pence

Create a shop window display. It need not have real things in it. Pin price tags to each item, and then set the children a number of tasks requiring them to make out bills and work out change.

The children can also convert prices to decimal notation and back again. They will need plenty of practice in doing this.

There are some money problems on **copymaster 21**.

Copymasters 22 (Shopping – track) and **23** (Shopping lists) make a board game. Photocopy on to card copymaster 23 and cut out these 'shopping lists'. Give one list and £3.50 in play money to each of three players. Let a fourth child be 'banker/shopkeeper' with a box of change and a calculator to check the players' spending. The winner is the first to buy all the items on their list (thereby spending all their money).

ZERO AND BELOW

Commentary

The concept of zero is familiar to children when they are very young. 'All gone' is in the vocabulary of most toddlers. Negative numbers are much more difficult to understand. One of the few ways we meet them in everyday life is in measuring temperature, and we have taken it as our example here.

One of the values in using a number line with children in their early number work is that its use can be extended below zero by counting backwards from a whole number.

Activity 1: Counting using zero

Use zero in all the oral counting you do with the children. For example, start their counts in 10s with zero, and their counts of children and experimental results. Add zero to all the number resources and charts available to the children.

Activity 2: Computation using zero

Use 0 in calculations you give to the children. Do not let their answers go below zero. Try to present as many different configurations of numbers as possible, giving

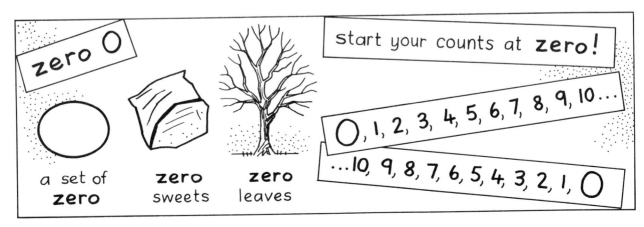

the children work in addition and subtraction, and including a variety of layouts, for example:

$$5 + 0 = ? \qquad 0 + 12 = ?$$

$$\begin{array}{r} 17 + \\ 0 \\ \hline \\ \hline \end{array}$$

$$16 - 0 = ? \qquad 4 - ? = 0$$

Activity 3: Calculators and zero
Point out that calculators always start you off at zero. Let the children use them to do, check and create calculations.

Activity 4: Looking at negative numbers
Show the children a freezer thermometer, and let them draw a picture of it, showing the scale. If possible, examine the thermometer while it is in a freezer and has a negative reading. Show the children a maximum and minimum thermometer. Let them draw and record the scale on that. If you can, record a night temperature of less than zero, so that they can see the thermometer in operation.

Let the children do an investigation into climate, to find out all they can. Their findings might include, for example:

- those areas of the world where the temperature is often below zero
- where people live at temperatures below zero
- the temperature of the coldest place on earth.

Make a *Negative Number Facts* book to add to a display or the book corner.

Activity 5: Making negative numbers
Show the children what happens when you subtract, for example, 7 from 5 using a calculator. Let the children create calculations involving negative numbers and record them in their books.

Copymaster 24 is a sheet of examples which can be done with or without a calculator, where some of the answers are negative numbers.

Programme of study: Number

Pupils should be taught to:

■ **3. Understanding relationships between numbers and developing methods of computation**

a use repeating patterns to develop ideas of regularity and sequencing;

Area of study	P of S	LD
13	3a	1

PATTERNS AROUND US

Commentary
The beginnings of algebra, like all other branches of mathematics, should start in the real world, and with the children themselves.

Activity 1: The children themselves
Let the children create repeat patterns using them-

selves and their classmates, lining up for all to see. Here are some examples:

- boy/girl/boy/girl/ ...
- with/without cardigans, long socks, white shirt or blouse, ...
- caterpillar patterns, like one arm/one leg/one arm/ ...

Let them try more sophisticated patterns, for example:

● two people with fair hair/two with dark hair/ . . .
● three five-year-olds/one six-year-old/ . . .
● one fan of 'Tom and Jerry'/one of 'Roadrunner'/ one of 'Mickey Mouse'/ . . .
● two people standing with arms up/one with arms down/ . . .

Activity 2: Everyday patterns

Encourage the children to look around the school and the immediate environment for patterns, both natural and designed. They may find things like patterns in brickwork and wallpaper, window sizes, plants in a garden border, railings, curtain designs, and floor tiles. In the natural world there are leaf attachment patterns, spots on ladybirds, ripples in a stream, branches on trees and flowers in blossom clusters. A range of patterns would make an impressive display, and could lead the children into other activities.

Activity 3: Pattern and human routines

Ask the children about the patterns in what they do every day. For example, 'wake up/get up/get dressed/ have breakfast/wash and clean teeth' may be one such routine. Look at routines in school, like 'register/ assembly/quiet reading/the order of work tasks/ play'. Discuss the patterns of meals in a day, hours in the day, days in a week, and other patterns that affect our everyday lives. Concertina books can be used to show a sequence, and children can be invited to say how their own routines vary from some examples.

Activity 4: Listening to patterns

The children can try describing or replicating patterns they hear. You can play recorded birdsong, sing songs with choruses, and listen to traffic noise and sounds of workmen digging up the road.

CREATING PATTERNS

Area of study 14 | P of S 3a | LD 1

Commentary

Pattern-making may not come after pattern investigation in children's intellectual development, for the noises and movements babies make and repeat may be early pattern-making rather than responses to the information their senses are giving them about the world. However, when the children have had plenty of opportunities to look at and for patterns, and to listen to patterns, they may be more adept at spotting pattern and creating more complex patterns themselves.

Arrange pattern-making activities so that they are as open-ended as possible, for, if a pre-set format is not imposed, there will be more variety in children's responses and greater learning opportunity available from the work of others.

When the children are asked to record pattern, in artwork or writing, they need to use techniques that get the pattern working quickly. For example, colouring in a repeat pattern of five red, then five yellow, then five blue beads, and repeating it again and again, may well outlast the enthusiasm of some children. If they can, say, print with red, yellow and blue potato cuts, the repeats will be done before the job becomes tedious.

When the children are skilful pattern-makers, look at the possibilities in 'orchestrating' their patterns. For example, how you display a set of painted patterns may demonstrate a rhythm which the children can tap out with sticks or shakers. A pattern of beads can translate into print on fabric. (See Activity 6, 'Pattern translation', on page 29.)

Activity 1: Human movement

During PE and dance sessions let the children work on movement sequences which have pattern. For example, to a tap on the tambour, the children can make a series of shapes in a sequence, returning to the start of the sequence when there are two quick taps.

'Machines' and 'Robots' are popular themes to explore, where movement routines can be repetitive and fun.

When the children have some movement routines developed, try getting them to work in pairs, first alongside one another, and then in pairs together. Keep the routines short, and let them watch each other's efforts and determine the patterns. If you want a record of the children's work, a set of photographs or tape of the children describing what they do would be a valuable addition to a display.

Activity 2: Making music

Make a music corner where the children can experiment with rhythm and sound patterns. Supply paper and pencil there too, so that they can experiment with ways to write down their patterns of 'music'.

When the children are gathered together and have a couple of minutes 'waiting time', try some clapping patterns, which they can copy.

Sing songs together, with repeats in the tune and in the words.

Activity 3: Patterns in words

Read poems which have a clear metre to the children. Let the children look for pairs of rhyming words and make up little rhymes to say. Sing the rhymes as a chant and try them as a round. Collect rhymes with rhythm for a class book.

Activity 4: Pattern in construction

Ask the children to create patterns with construction toys, including Lego®, wooden bricks, plastic straws, Duplo®, coloured Plasticine® and spent matches.

Activity 5: Pattern in artwork

Here are a few of the many possibilities. Colour, paint and draw blobs, triangles, beads on necklaces, buttons on jackets, stripes on snakes, rungs on ladders, stripes on trousers and tigers; print with hands, fingers and feet, boxes and other junk, potatoes and string, to make friezes, borders, book covers, drapes, and wrapping paper; made collages with repeat shapes in paper, card, cellophane, fabric, wool; construct paper chains, mobiles and towers from art materials.

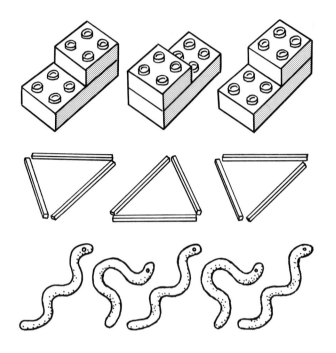

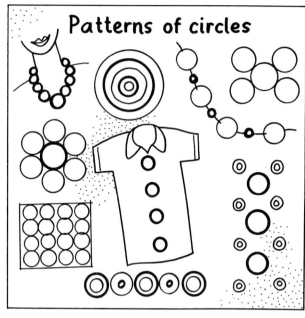

Activity 6: Pattern translation

Try getting the children to use a pattern format in several ways. For example, they might invent a pattern with bricks, tap out that pattern on the drum, paint the pattern in stripes, and sign the pattern with coloured strokes on a piece of paper. Arrange a tempting display where the children can 'translate' each other's patterns into other modes of presentation.

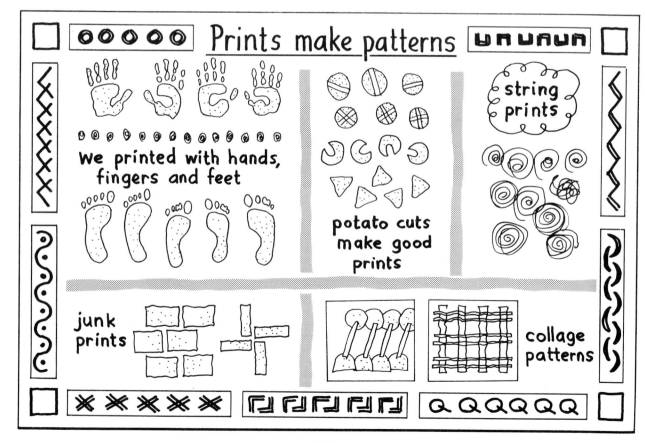

28

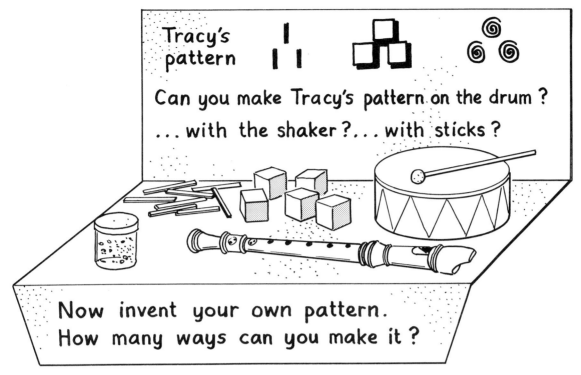

Activity 7: Patterns of numerals

The children will be familiar with counting rhymes and numbers in sequence in their work on AT 2 Number. Let them record a pattern they can see, using numerals.

Next ask the children to create patterns using numerals, then to use these in their music or artwork.

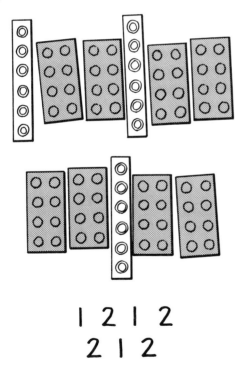

 PLAYING WITH PATTERNS

Commentary

There are many ways of increasing children's awareness of and sensitivity to pattern. We have listed some here. They could be seen as extension activities.

Until now we have not set children patterns to copy,

continue or complete. This is because over-prescription can stifle creativity. If the children have had plenty of practice in the previous activities, then they can sometimes now be given a pattern to replicate.

Activity 1: A pattern-crazy day

Designate a day as, for example, a 1 2 1 2 day, and ask the children to try to bring the pattern into their tasks for the day (without going to extremes!). For example, they can pin a note on the door, saying 'Please give a KNOCK knock knock KNOCK knock knock'. Their maths can be related to numbers and shapes in these patterns. Their music-making can match the pattern. Their artwork can be based on this too. In dance or PE they can invent a march or a gymnastics routine based on the same 1 2 1 2 pattern. Home corner play can use the pattern; in serving up play dinner, the cook can give out one potato, two potatoes, and so on. At the end of the day, you should have a wealth of material for a display or an assembly – and all from one simple repeat pattern.

Activity 2: A pattern quiz

Give the children a set of patterns to look for. You can confine them to the classroom, or the school block, or you can let them take the quizzes home.

An example quiz is set out on **copymaster 25** (Patterns around you).

Activity 3: Repeat and try out

Try out some 'What comes next?' and 'What is after that?' patterns with the children.

Try setting up a pattern which the children have to continue and then test out. For example, a 3 1 2 4 pattern might be laid out in blocks or signed as dots on paper. The children can continue it and play the pattern on a percussion instrument or clap the pattern to see if it is correct.

Copymaster 26 (Number patterns) is a sheet of patterns to continue and check.

Programme of study: Number

Pupils should be taught to:

- **3. Understanding relationships between numbers and developing methods of computation**

  b explore and record patterns in addition and subtraction, and then patterns of multiples, *eg 3, 6, 9, 12*, explaining their patterns and using them to make predictions; progress to exploring further patterns involving multiplication and division, including those within a hundred-square of multiplication facts;

Area of study 16	P of S 3b	LD 2

PATTERNS IN ADDITION/SUBTRACTION TO 10

 C27

Commentary

The children should do this work in conjunction with their work on number. In fact, if they have had much practice in pattern-making, they will *expect* there to be a pattern in their number work.

In looking at number–algebra links, there are two important considerations. In tackling any mathematics activity it is vital not to see it in isolation from other areas of the curriculum, or from other areas of mathematics. Only through making explicit the links and interdependence between mathematical topics will we help the children to become numerate.

Activity 1: Make a number

As you and the children work through a range of activities related to each of the numerals to 10, let them use a variety of counting aids to make patterns of each number. Include among these pattern sets those made 'in steps' with Unifix®, Multilink® or similar apparatus.

Let the children use sticky paper shapes, colouring and printing to replicate these patterns. Make a display of the children's work. Numerals can be attached to the patterns made, to show addition and subtraction bonds.

```
Patterns of 7

1 O                  X X X X X X X          1 2 3 4 5 6 7    | 0 | 7 |
2 O O                  X X X X X X ⌂        □ □ □ □ □ □ □    | 1 | 6 |
3 O O O                  X X X X X ⌂ ⌂      □ □ □ □ □ □      | 2 | 5 |
4 O O O O                  X X X X ⌂ ⌂ ⌂    □ □ □ □ □        | 3 | 4 |
5 O O O O O                  X X X ⌂ ⌂ ⌂ ⌂  □ □ □ □          | 4 | 3 |
6 O O O O O O                  X X ⌂ ⌂ ⌂ ⌂ ⌂ □ □ □           | 5 | 2 |
7 O O O O O O O                  X ⌂ ⌂ ⌂ ⌂ ⌂ ⌂ □ □            | 6 | 1 |
                                 ⌂ ⌂ ⌂ ⌂ ⌂ ⌂ ⌂  □            | 7 | 0 |
```

Activity 2: Finish the pattern

Present children with patterned sequences of number bonds, where they have to complete the pattern or fill in the missing numbers. If they have mastered the steps in making numbers to 10 they should do these very quickly.

There are patterns of this kind to complete on **copymaster 27** (Number bonds).

```
Make 6    5 + 1 =
          4 + 2 =
          3 + 3 =
          2 + 4 =
          1 + 5 =
```

Area of study 17	P of S 3b	LD 2	**PATTERN EXPLANATION AND PREDICTION**	C28

Commentary

The aim is that children should have a knowledge of number facts to 10, to the point where they can say them almost 'without thinking', or can work them out quickly, from their knowledge of the patterns formed by addition and subtraction to 10.

Class books and charts of number patterns should have as much appeal as poems or pictures. Do not deprive children of the pleasure of number by confining the patterns to worksheets or exercise books.

Activity 1: Oral number patterns

Quick-fire questions to the whole group, or individuals within it, will help the children to work out patterns in number facts to 10. Here are some examples:

● 'Today we are going to make seven. I shall give you a number and you can call out what we need to add to make seven. 0 . . . 1 . . . 2 . . . 3 . . . 4 . . . 5 . . . 6 . . . 7 . . . 3 . . . 2 . . . 5 . . . 6', and so on.

● 'Do some "take away 2" calculations in your head. I shall say a number and you call out what that number less 2 is. 10 . . . 9 . . . 8 . . . 7 . . . 6 . . . 5 . . . (etc.) . . . 10 . . . 8 . . . 6 . . . 4', and so on.

● 'Give me a way of making 6 . . . and another . . . and another. Now make 6 using subtraction.'

Activity 2: Pattern layouts

Give the children the chance to record all the possible ways to make all the numbers up to 10, using addition and subtraction. It may be a good idea to have a class book of these.

If you have space for a 'number corner' you could use number patterns as one topic for a regular display. Mobiles, number strings, flap surprises, feely bags are some of the possible ways of displaying these.

Copymaster 28 presents some number pattern arrays for children to complete.

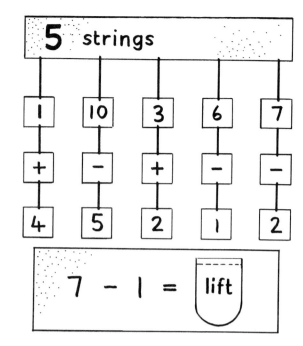

| Area of study 18 | P of S 3b | LD 2 | | **NUMBER PATTERNS TO 100** | C3–5, 29, 30, R2–4 |

Commentary

Mathematics is about patterns. Much of the fun to be found in maths is in the patterns that occur and that we can make with numbers, or through using numbers. Many adults who feel they are no good at maths are people who have never been shown that patterns in maths are as beautiful as patterns in language and art. It is important to say this because a liking or disliking for maths is in the hands of teachers of young children. It is vital that the children and their parents begin to see that maths is not just 'sums' and sometimes has little to do with sums.

Activity 1: Making patterns

Make patterns of numbers up to and including ten,

with Unifix® or Multilink®, sticky shapes, a ten by ten square drawn on large squared paper, or beads on a string. If the children have good hand control skills, they could draw graphs of number bonds to ten.

Resource copymaster R4 is a page of large squares.

Activity 2: Inventing patterns

Ask the children to create patterns which involve counting to ten. Some of these may demonstrate bonds to ten. Encourage the children to devise short ways of describing the patterns they create, using maths symbols. Here are some possibilities.

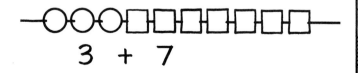

3 + 7

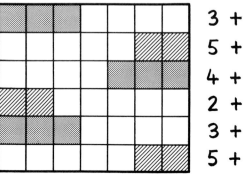

3 + 4
5 + 2
4 + 3
2 + 5
3 + 4
5 + 2

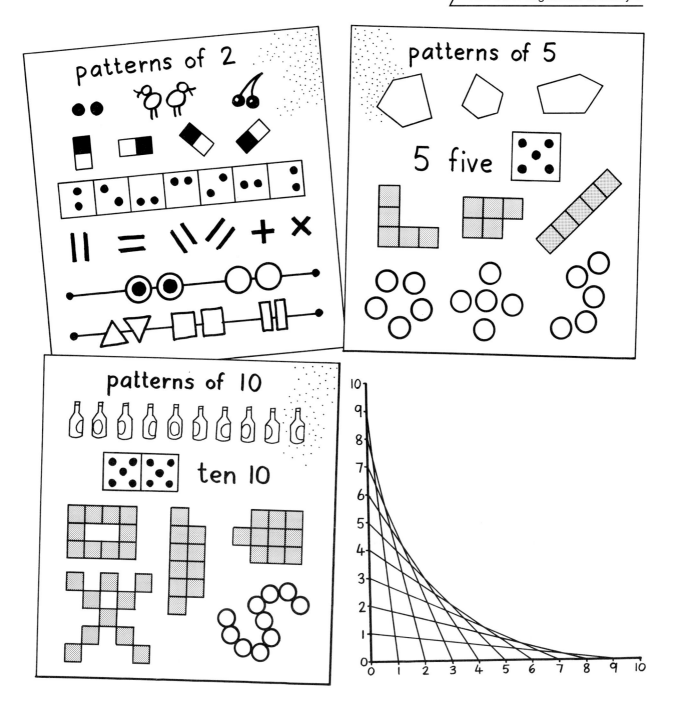

Activity 3: Oral counting

Here are games to play with a group or the whole class in a spare few minutes. Let all the children count aloud up to 10, up to 20, up to 30, . . . and eventually up to 100.

Then start the counts at numbers other than 1, like this: 'Count from 26 to 43', 'Count from 17 to 52'.

Make the game more complicated by saying things like: 'I want you to count together, up to 40. Each time you say a number which is written with a '1' in it, clap your hands.' The first twelve numbers will be like this:

1 (clap), 2, 3, 4, 5, 6, 7, 8, 9, **10** (clap), **11** (clap), **12** (clap), . . .

Next introduce clapping for '3s' then '5s'.

Keep the counting short and snappy, for the children will soon get in a muddle if their concentration breaks. When they are good at counting as a class, ask some to listen while other small groups or pairs do the counting.

Try asking the children to say aloud the answers to questions like the following:

- What is the next number after 16?
- What is one more than 74?
- What is two more than 11?
- Which is the bigger number, 23 or 12?
- Which is smaller, 78 or 87?
- Which is biggest, 33, 45 or 56?
- Which is smallest, 2, 15 or 10?

Activity 4: Play with 100

Play counting in tens, counting backwards in tens, and colouring hundred squares in a variety of ways. The hundred square is a device that can be returned to

33

again and again, in cyclical fashion, as the children master place value, and begin to work with larger numbers.

Here is a typical sequence of tasks for a child to do, over a period of days or weeks:

● Colour the pattern of counting in ones (that is, every square!).
● Colour the pattern of counting in tens.
● Colour all the numbers with a 3 in them (or 4, or any digit).
● Fill in the numbers on a blank ten by ten square.
● Fill in the numbers on a blank ten by ten square and then colour the important numbers to them. (They may include their age, the number of brothers and sisters they have, the number of their house and so on.)

The purpose here is to encourage the children to play around with the hundred square until they are thoroughly familiar with it. Note that the patterns of two, five, and other numbers will be considered at Level 3 where the hundred square can be used again. See Area of study 20.

There are hundred squares on **resource copymasters R2** and **R3**.

Activity 5: Counting games
Let the children play games like 'Snakes and ladders', which is actually a number track and not a hundred square, but nevertheless will get them looking at and calling out numbers to 100. You (or the children) can invent other track games.

There are unnumbered track games on **copymasters 9** (Ladybird race), **4** (Cheese chase) and **15** (Home time!) and numbered ones on **copymasters 29** (Leap frog) and **30** (Planes and parachutes).

TWOS, FIVES AND TENS

| Area of study 19 | P of S 3b | LD 3 |

Commentary
This work ties in with that in P of S 3c. The work on both parts of the Programme of study could be done at the same time.

The emphasis here is on the pattern of the numbers, and so it could be reinforced through pattern-making in art.

Activity 1: Multiply/divide by 2
Immerse the children in the pattern of twos. Have a pattern-making day and produce towers of twos, constructions of two strips/bricks, border patterns of twos, collage in twos, printing in twos, an ark and animals in twos. Make a '2' display and *The Story of 2* classbook.

Fill a resource box called 'Fun to do with 2', which could include colouring with shades of two colours, finding out about two kinds of big cat, asking two people with different views about what happens to grandma in Red Riding Hood, and creating birthday cakes for a second birthday.

Activity 2: 'Two' rhymes
Collect these and teach them to the children. Include rhymes like 'Ten fat sausages' and 'Two, four, six, eight, who do we appreciate?'

Activity 3: Multiply/divide by 5
Repeat similar activities as Activity 1 above, including things like printing, collage and borders. Use squared paper (5 by 10 squares) to make patterns (**resource copymasters R4** and **R5** are for squared paper). Ask the children to invent rhymes and stories 'all about five'.

34

Activity 4: Multiply/divide by 10

Treat 10 in the way 2 and 5 are handled in Activities 1 and 3. Use hundred squares (**resource copymasters R2 and R3**), coinage and notes, a Celsius thermometer scale, and number lines to highlight the pattern of tens.

Activity 5: Calculator play

Let the children make patterns of 2, 5, and 10 on the calculator.

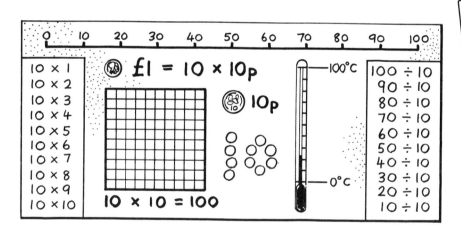

| Area of study 20 | P of S 3b | LD 3 | **PATTERNS OF MULTIPLES** | CR2, R3 |

Commentary

Having worked on patterns of twos, fives and tens (see Area of study 19) the children can continue to work on number patterns and place these on hundred squares (see **copymasters R2, R3**).

Activity 1: Multiply/divide by 3, 4 and more

Repeat similar activities to those in Area of study 19 activities 1–5 making patterns of counting in threes and fours. Then try pattern making with 6, 7, 8 and 9.

Activity 2: Hundred square patterns

Use hundred square grids like those on **copymasters R2 and R3** to allow the children to colour patterns of

counting in twos, fives, tens, threes, fours and so on. Discuss with them the outcomes. Let the children look for numbers which occur in more than one pattern. Let them also look carefully at the configuration of each pattern. For example some patterns make vertical 'stripes' (*eg 2, 5, 10*). Some diagonal (*eg 3*) and some offset ⬜ ⬜ ⬜ ⬜ like this (*eg 4*).

Activity 3: Multiplication square

Ask the children to complete a 10×10 square filling in the products of each multiplication as shown here. Point out to the children that the square has a line of symmetry along the diagonal.

×	1	2	3	4	5	6	7	8	9	10
1	1	2	3	4	5	6	7	8	9	10
2	2	4	6	8	10	12	14	16	18	20
3	3	6	9	12	15	18	21	24	27	30
4	4	8	12	16	20	24	28	32	36	40
5	5	10	15	20	25	30	35	40	45	50
6	6	12	18	24	30	36	42	48	54	60
7	7	14	21	28	35	42	49	56	63	70
8	8	16	24	32	40	48	56	64	72	80
9	9	18	27	36	45	54	63	72	81	90
10	10	20	30	40	50	60	70	80	90	100

← line of symmetry

Programme of study: Number

Pupils should be taught to:

■ **3. Understanding relationships between numbers and developing methods of computation**

c know addition and subtraction facts to 20, and develop a range of mental methods for finding, from known facts, those that they cannot recall; learn multiplication and division facts relating to the 2s, 5s, 10s, and use these to learn other facts, *eg double multiples of 2 to produce multiples of 4*, and to develop mental methods for finding new results;

Area of study 21	P of S 3c	LD 1

BEGINNING ADDITION ▶

Commentary

Aim for 100% success. We need confident mathematicians! This will require taking the children forward a step at a time, because then you can pick up a problem the first time it occurs, and not have a child experience repeated failure.

It is important that you are able to oversee each child, so place the children in small ability groups with flexible membership.

As in 'Beginning counting', the children themselves are their own and your first resource.

In putting several more objects into a set, as in Activities 1 to 3 opposite, the children are in fact adding two sets together – that is, the original set and however many more.

In setting out the first sets for them to combine, try to practise the left to right across the page layout, with the answer on the right. Not all sums are arranged like this, but much early number work depends on this kind of presentation. We do not want children to feel they do not understand maths simply because they do not understand the way it appears on the page.

There are lots of words in use in computation discussion. Use the words that you find familiar at first. Tell the children about the words you do not use regularly, when you feel they are ready.

36

Activity 1: And one more child makes . . .

From a group, name three children to stand up. Let the children count how many are standing. Ask another to stand and say '. . . and one more makes . . . ?' Do this again and again, getting the named children to sit down, stand on one leg, put their hands in the air, and so on. Then increase the number you add to the set, ensuring that the final total does not exceed ten. ('Estimation' Activity 3 has links with this activity.)

Activity 2: And one more thing makes . . .

Ask each child in a group to collect a given number of objects. Go around the group, asking how many objects each child has. From a handful of things that you have yourself, add one more to each set and say '. . . and one more makes . . . ?' Let each child assemble different numbers of things in their 'set', and play this out many times. Let each child have a go as 'teacher' while you become a member of the group.

Some traditional stories are useful here, for the children can count '. . . and one more makes . . .' as each person is added to the story.

Repeat the activity many times, adding a greater number of items to each set, but ensuring the final set size does not go above ten. The children can take turns at displaying their counts, and what happens when one more is added.

Activity 3: Recording

Give the children pictures on which to match, draw and record additions to sets.

Activity 4: Putting sets together

Let the children lay out two separate sets, count each, and then physically combine them to give a total count. Play with a group, doing this several times yourself, and then letting each child have a go.

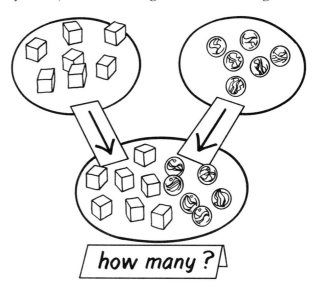

Activity 5: Practical addition

Let children make up their own collections of objects which they count and combine. Remember to give them chances to add more than two small sets. You can limit their choices by supplying numerals on cards of different colours. The children choose numerals of different colours, collect those numbers of objects, and then combine the sets, finding the numeral corresponding to the count of the combined sets.

Activity 6: Addition language

Here are some of the words children need to know, even if they do not use them themselves: 'addition', 'add', 'plus', 'the sum of', 'total', 'makes'. There is also much language they will have met during earlier counting activities, including: 'more', 'most', 'less', 'least', 'bigger', 'smaller', and so on. Encourage the children to talk about numbers using this vocabulary. Use these words in displays, flashcards and work tasks.

37

Area of study 22	P of S 3c	LD 1	**FIRST ADDITIONS**

Commentary

When you are preparing maths work with non-maths words in it, give the children a picture–word code sheet. They should then have a chance to do the maths rather than spending all their time trying to find out what the words mean!

Activity 1: Picture recording

Let the children assemble two sets of things and put the two sets together, as in 'Beginning addition' above, then ask them to draw in their books what they did. When they can record what they have done practically, you can give them some picture recording problems which are partly drawn already.

Activity 2: Addition

Give the children additions with words like 'plus' or 'add' and 'equals' in them. For example:

● 4 cats add 2 cats equals ___ cats altogether.
● 3 oranges plus 1 orange makes ___ oranges.

The children should do plenty of these, using all combinations of number to ten. Include some like this:

● 1 sock add 4 socks add 5 socks makes ___ socks.

You can draw pictures to make these more inviting, but the children should use counting aids as and when they need them. All the objects for the count do not have to be drawn in.

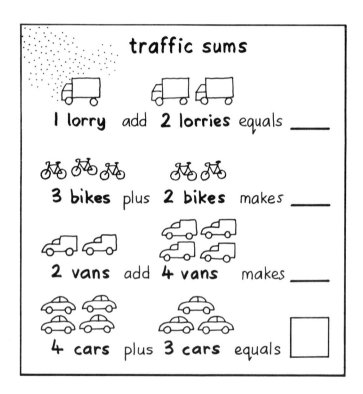

38

Area of study 23 | P of S 3c | LD 1

BEGINNING SUBTRACTION

 C31

Commentary

You may choose to wait until the children are competent at addition before introducing subtraction. You could do both operations alongside one another, or subtraction first if you wish. The important point is that addition and subtraction are related, and the children should be helped to understand this.

It could be argued that subtraction is more familiar to young children because they have plenty of experience of having things 'taken away' from them before they reach school age! However, what they may not have a sense of is the connection between 'take aways' and 'adds'. For example: $2 + 3 = 5$, $5 - 2 = 3$, $5 - 3 = 2$.

Once more it is important to remember aspects of language: 'take away', 'minus', 'less than' and so on.

Activity 1: Take me away!

From a group, ask a number of children to stand at the front. Count how many there are and then physically take one child away, and ask how many are left. Do this repeatedly with different participants, taking two away, then three, eventually trying all patterns of take away possible with the group.

Activity 2: Take away objects

Repeat Activity 1 using things belonging to the children, for example, PE bags, pumps, cardigans, shoes, pencil cases and other things available. Then work with things around the room, and pictures of things.

take away 1   how many left ?

Activity 3: Take away strips

Using rubber stamp pictures, those you have drawn yourself, or some cut from a catalogue, make a series of pictures along a strip of card. Make little cuts between the pictures so that they can be flapped up and down.

39

Use the strips with the children to play take aways, setting up the starting number of birds on the wall or buns in the shop, or whatever the pictures depict. Flap down out of sight the number taken away, and count those left. If you find it helpful, you could make a large take away strip, to use with a group of children.

Copymaster 31 (Take away strips) provides two ready made examples.

Activity 4: Take away rhymes

Teach the children songs and rhymes like 'Ten green bottles', 'Five speckled frogs', 'Five little ducks went swimming one day', 'There were ten in the bed', 'Poor Jane Higgins, she had five piggins' and 'Five little monkeys walked along the shore'. Make a copy of some rhymes in a homemade book for the book corner.

Area of study	P of S	LD	
24	**3c**	**1**	**FIRST SUBTRACTIONS** ▶

Commentary

Take care with the concept of subtraction! People often see subtraction as being about taking away or about the difference between two things. There are both language difficulties bound up in these concepts and a difference in direction between the two views. 'Less than' implies a 'more to less' direction, but the difference notion can be described as being in either direction.

In the children's experience, for example in corner shops, many adults solve subtractions by adding on. This is an important approach and one which you need to be aware of in giving the children the vocabulary of subtraction. But beware of too narrow an adherence to standard methods! It is important for the children to be able to offer personal methods too. Explanations of personal methods are often good ways of exploring underlying concepts.

Activity 1: Practical take aways

As in 'Beginning addition' Activity 5 and 'First additions' Activity 1 above, the children should now set up their own take aways, laying out a number of toys, picture recording how many, and then actually taking some away to find how many left, and drawing them.

Activity 2: Subtraction language

Discuss with the children the words used in talking about 'take aways', including 'subtract', 'minus' and 'take'. Make up a group take away story, and display a picture version.

Activity 3: Subtraction

Give the children written subtractions with words like 'take away' and 'left over' written in. For example:

- 6 carrots take away 1 carrot. __ carrots left over.
- 9 mice take away 5 mice leaves __ mice.

As with additions at this stage, pictures will make the subtractions more inviting, but the children should use counting aids as and when they need them. All the objects at the start or finish do not need to be drawn in.

The story of 5 buns	I fell off the plate...	I was eaten by Marcus...
Once there were 5 buns	...then there were 4	...only 3 left
	5 minus 1 equals 4	4 subtract 1

40

Area of study 25	P of S 3c	LD 2

ADDITION AND SUBTRACTION

C29,30, 32,33 R1

Commentary

Teachers often let children use workcards and worksheets to do pages of 'sums'. There are some points to consider.

● Why are the children doing these calculations?
● Are patterns in number preserved, where possible, in the order the calculations are presented?
● Are the workcards and worksheets ideal in layout and condition? (We have all seen children working on sheets that make little sense to the teacher, let alone the children, and using workcards that are 15 years old, and look it.)

It may be that many children become disinterested in maths when they are forced to rehearse skills they already have. They consequently spend less time on those aspects of maths that are so useful in everyday life, like estimation, approximation and problem solving. In this respect it is necessary to look at how schemes are being used. It is the teacher and the children who should set the mathematics agenda, not the writers of a scheme. Schemes are not substitutes for school development plans, they are resources which should be employed as and when necessary. There is nothing more destructive of children's mathematical development than to make them work through a scheme regardless of individual strengths and insights!

There is a need here to be clear about the previous experiences of the children. If they are moving to Level 2 work within the year, then you should find this no problem. However, if this represents a transition of

class as well as year, then it is important to establish what the child knows in terms of their language experience.

At Level 2, symbols are used as 'shorthand' for important mathematical operations and relationships. It is important to be consistent in using these, while still allowing children to develop personal methods for problem solution.

Activity 1: Addition: the 'plus' and 'equals' signs

Discuss with the children the signs for 'add' and 'equals'. Give them numeral cards and some with '+' or '=', and watch them make the start of a calculation and transfer it to their books. This activity should be used as a bridge from Level 1 work.

$$2 \quad + \quad 5 \quad = \quad \square$$

$$1 \quad + \quad \square \quad = \quad 4$$

Activity 2: Additions

Now that the children have met all the appropriate vocabulary and know what to expect, they should be given plenty of opportunities to record additions to ten. Both layout and vocabulary should be varied in the presentation of the calculations.

$$7 + 1 = \square$$
$$8 + 2 = \square$$
$$5 + 5 = \square$$
$$4 + \square = 5$$
$$\square + 1 = 6$$

2 add 3 makes □

5 plus 4 equals □

make 10

add 4 and ____

2 and ____

Activity 3: Addition dice games

When playing track games like 'Snakes and ladders', to make the game move quickly and reinforce number bonds, the children could play with two dice with the 6 deleted (so that totals do not exceed ten), summing the two numbers before they make a move. Use commercial track games and those you make yourself. Make dice or spinners which use the numbers 6 to 9. For example, the children could play with a pair of spinners, where one has 3 to 8 and the other has 1s and 2s. (**Resource copymaster R1** includes blank spinners for you to use here.)

Activity 4: Addition card games

Make some addition games, using, for example, bonds to five or ten. The game can be like 'Bingo' or simply a set of cards with numbers on them which an individual or two children can assemble into patterns of five or ten.

The games for two players on **copymasters 32** (Make five) and **33** (Make ten) can be used in this way. Photocopy each copymaster on to card, and cut out the game cards. Share the cards between the players. In 'Make five', the players take turns to put down cards which make a total of five in any combination. In 'Make ten', they take turns to make patterns of ten (six and four etc.). For both games the winner is the player with fewest (or no) cards left.

Activity 5: Addition using a calculator

Let the children check their answers to additions by using a calculator. Then ask them to make up additions on the calculator and write them out with the answers. They can give the additions to friends to do, without letting them see the answers.

Activity 6: Subtraction: the 'minus' and 'equals' signs

Discuss with the children the signs for '−' and '=' (they have already met the equals sign in addition). Make cards with the minus sign on them and use them with the cards for Activity 1 'Addition: the "plus" and "equals" signs'. Let the children set out a subtraction using numeral cards and the sign cards before transferring it to their book.

Activity 7: Subtractions

The children should have plenty of opportunity to record subtractions to ten. Both layout and vocabulary should be varied in the presentation of subtractions.

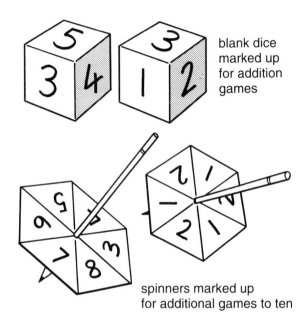

blank dice marked up for addition games

spinners marked up for additional games to ten

There are track games on **copymasters 29** (Leap frog) and **30** (Planes and parachutes).

8 − 4 = ☐

7 − 3 = ☐

10 − 2 = __

6 − ☐ = 2

☐ − 1 = 7

9− 6− 7− 8−
5   3   2   6
__   __   __   __
__   __   __   __

7 take away 4 leaves ☐

5 minus 2 equals ☐

3 subtract 1 equals ___

The difference between 5 and 2 is ___

Activity 8: Dice games

Let the children play track games using two dice. Before they move, they subtract the smaller number from the bigger number shown on the dice or spinners. Vary the spinners and dice, so that the children can practise all subtraction possibilities, within 10.

The track games on **copymasters 29** (Leap frog) and **30** (Planes and parachutes) may be adapted in this way.

Activity 9: Subtraction using a calculator

As in Activity 5, 'Addition using a calculator', let the children check their answers using a calculator, and then set subtractions for their friends, using the calculator to mark answers.

Activity 10: Oral work on number bonds

When you have a couple of minutes with the class, between sessions or activities, give them some quick-fire oral work. For example:

● Let's make 5. What do I need to make 5? 1 and what? 2 and what?
● Let's make 10. 7 and what? 9 and what? 1 and 4 and what?
● The answer I want is 2. I have 8 buns. How many must I eat to have only 2 left? What if I start with 3 buns?
● I start with 5 marbles. If I lose 2, how many are left?

Activity 11: Think of a number

Give the children a number, for example, 26. Go around the class, asking what can they tell you about that number. You may get things like:

● It is written 2 and 6.
● It has 2 tens.
● The other way round it would be 62.
● $2 + 6 = 8$, $6 + 2 = 8$, $6 - 2 = 4$.
● My birthday is 26 May.
● My mum is 26.

● My cousin lives at number 26.
● 2 is a swan swimming and 6 is a swan sleeping.
● There are 26 letters in the alphabet.

Now let the children choose a number and investigate it in a small group setting.

blank dice marked up
for subtraction games

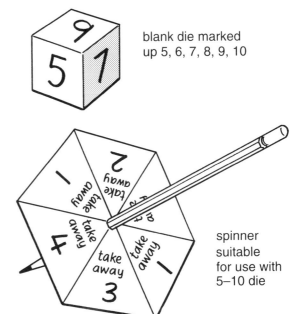

blank die marked
up 5, 6, 7, 8, 9, 10

spinner
suitable
for use with
5–10 die

| Area of study 26 | P of S 3c | LD 2 | **ADDITION AND SUBTRACTION TO 20** | C34,35, R5 |

Commentary

The children should have mastered all the addition and subtraction facts to 10 at Level 2. Now they need to extend that knowledge to 20. Through rehearsal of computation, using counting aids, and recording their efforts, they should be able to commit important number bonds to memory. This is not rote learning, if they fully understand what is happening to the numbers.

Now is the time to establish 'zero' in the children's calculations. Activities relating to this concept and negative numbers are discussed in 'Zero and below' in this section.

In moving from number facts which should be memorised to the manipulation of 'sums' on paper, there is a tendency to teach children a standard method (algorithm) for doing those calculations. It is important to be circumspect about teaching such algorithms. There are a variety of standard algorithms and not one best method; children's own methods need exploration, and teaching children to 'crack a code' has to be matched with their understanding.

Activity 1: Patterns

The children can make patterns of number to 20 on small squared paper. There is a sheet of centimetre squares on **resource copymaster R5**.

The children can use Unifix®, Multilink®, Colour Factor® or other counting aids, and set out the pattern of bonds to 20. **Copymaster 34** (Subtraction bonds to 20) is a practice sheet.

Activity 2: Rehearsing and checking

Do not make children do pages and pages of 'sums', in the hope that number bonds to 20 will be absorbed. Try as many different ways of presenting them as you can think of, including, for example, the following:

● Check your answers on the calculator.
● Mark your friend's answers.
● Check your friend's answers on the calculator.
● List all the calculations that you can think of with the numbers 2 and 12 in them.
● Start with $10 + 2 = ?$. Underneath it write another calculation where only one of the figures is one more or one less than before. Do this again and again until you have done all you can.
● Create calculations with two ten-sided dice.

Activity 3: Oral addition and subtraction

Spend a couple of minutes each day in oral number work, so that, as quick as a flash, the children can eventually do the following:

● Compute in their heads, all the bonds to make exactly 20; for example, 6 and 14, 10 and 10.

● Compute in their heads all the subtraction facts to 20; for example, 20 minus 2 is 18.
● Know all about addition and subtraction within 20; for example, that $5 + 3 + 7 = 15$ and that 11 can be made up of a range of numbers including, for example, 4, 4 and 3.

Activity 4: Addition and subtraction games

Make up 'Bingo' and 'Snap' cards to play games using number bonds to 20.

A suitable game is given on **copymaster 35** (Bingo). You may like to ask the children to make their own, which they can play at home.

Photocopy copymaster 35 on to card, then cut out the four base cards. Cut out the numerals and put them in a box. Four players take a base card each. A 'caller' takes a numeral out of the box and calls it out. The first player to find an addition or subtraction on their base card to which the number is the answer is given the numeral, and covers the calculation. The winner is the first player to cover their base card.

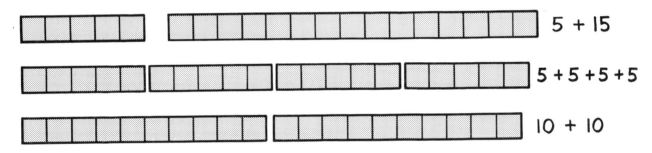

<table>
<tr><td>Area of study 27</td><td>P of S 3c</td><td>LD 3</td></tr>
</table>

► BEGINNING MULTIPLICATION ►

Commentary

Multiplication and division are generally regarded as being much more difficult operations for children to understand than addition and subtraction. The links that adults may see between, for example, multiplication and repeated addition, are not obvious to children and lots of varied work will be needed to forge such links.

Multiplication and division are inextricably linked. However, because we think it is easier to tackle one kind of work with numbers at a time, we have chosen to introduce them to the children separately. It is important to make links, when the children understand both operations.

It is a moot point as to whether the teaching of multiplication should precede the teaching of division. 'Sharing' is often more common in the previous experience of children. It is worth considering using some 'sharing' talk alongside your early work in multiplication.

Activity 1: Playing 'lots of'

This kind of play demands a special resource box which has a number of toys and other items displaying

features to be included in 'lots of' counting. Include things like these:

model people (2s – legs and arms)
socks (2s – pairs)
mittens or gloves (2s – pairs)
2p coins (2s)
triangles (3s – sides and corners)
model milking stools (3s – legs)
three-bead necklaces (3s – beads)
model animals (4s – legs)
model cars (4s – wheels)
bunches of paper flowers (5s – flowers in each bunch)
5p coins (5s)
egg boxes (6s – eggs)
10p coins (10s).

Using such a resource bank the children will be able to grasp the concept of a 'lot'. Remind them that they can use their knowledge of number patterns to work out the total in a number of 'lots'.

The children can then set out repeated displays of 'lots of' using their own display cards, or ones that you have made for them.

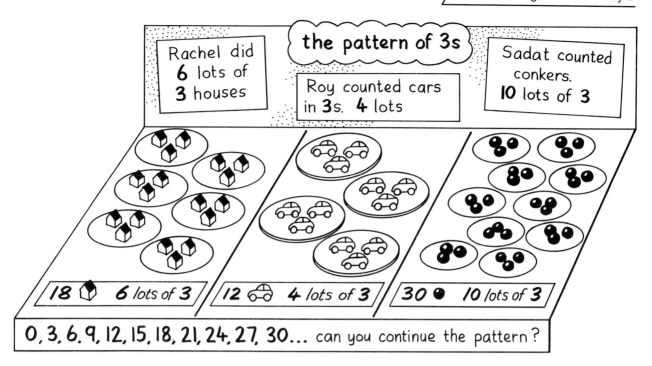

the pattern of 3s

Rachel did **6** lots of **3** houses

Roy counted cars in **3**s. **4** lots

Sadat counted conkers. **10** lots of **3**

18 🏠 6 *lots of 3* 12 🚗 4 *lots of 3* 30 ● 10 *lots of 3*

0, 3, 6, 9, 12, 15, 18, 21, 24, 27, 30... can you continue the pattern?

Activity 2: Picture 'lots of'

Let the children record in their books, the results of some picture 'lots of' sums. This could include a 'mountain' of 3s or a tower of 5s.

It can be helpful for the children to recreate the number patterns in 'lots of' and put them into a little book, which they can keep. It is a 'tables' book in disguise! Class charts can be created too.

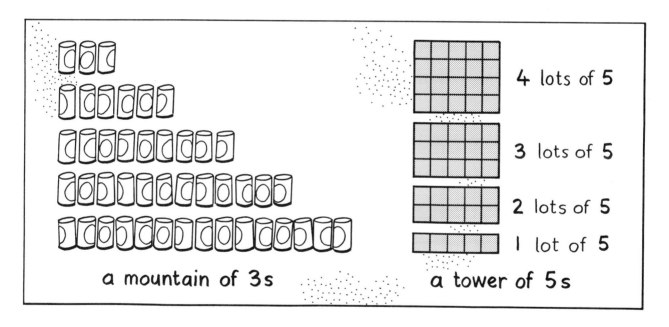

a mountain of 3s

4 lots of 5

3 lots of 5

2 lots of 5

1 lot of 5

a tower of 5s

| Area of study 28 | P of S 3c | LD 3 | **FIRST MULTIPLICATIONS** | C36–39, R1 |

Commentary

Now that the children are beyond the stage of being starter mathematicians, they should be able to take the step from talking about 'lots of' to 'times' quite readily.

Again you should be wary of introducing a particular standard algorithm as *the* way to do multiplications. For many children the algorithm can assume more importance than the concept of multiplication.

Activity 1: Practical 'times' calculations

Using the resource bank from 'Beginning multiplication' Activity 1, the children can set out and talk you through their maths. Note that, from saying things like '3 lots of legs', you can encourage them to move towards saying things like '3 lots of 2'. They can match what they have done to an appropriate problem card, which also has all the counting information on it.

Activity 2: 'Times' language and sign

Use 'times', 'multiply' and the sign '✕' with the children, and add them to the maths language book or chart in class.

Activity 3: Multiplications

These need to involve larger numbers for children to see the pattern in multiplication. Give them number patterns where they fill in what is missing. **Copymaster 36** (Missing numbers) is a sheet of such puzzles.

Use all your ingenuity to create and recreate multiplication bonds, using a variety of layouts and vocabulary and dice, including a blank one on which you can write the mathematical signs.

Activity 4: Multiplication using the calculator

As with addition and subtraction, calculators are invaluable for marking, checking and setting multiplications, and checking out patterns of number.

Activity 5: Oral multiplication

Practise tables! The tables mean nothing unless the children understand what they are doing with the numbers, but it is an asset to know, apparently without thinking, that 36 follows 27 in a pattern of 9s, for example. Try these:

● Start a pattern and see if the children can detect what the next but one number will be – 0, 3, 6, 9, ?, ? (answer 15)
● Give a 'middle' of the pattern and see if the children can 'count down' in the pattern as well as up – 26, 24, 22, 20, ? (answer 18, 16, 14, 12)

Activity 6: Multiplying games

The same sorts of games can be used for multiplying as for other operations. 'Bingo' and 'Snap' are applicable.

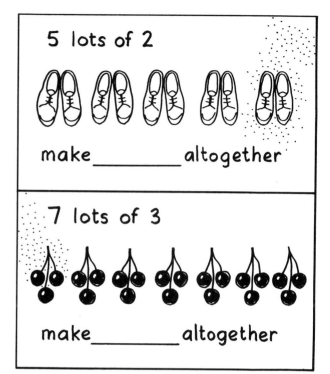

Board games need to be ingenious to avoid the winner reaching the end in one mighty bound!

Copymasters 37 and **38** (Zap!) make a multiplication board game for two to four players. Photocopy copymaster 38 on to card, and cut out the multiplication cards. Place them face down in a pile. The players throw an ordinary die in turn, moving their counter as usual. If they land on a 'Zap' square, they turn over the top card and work out the multiplication, the other players checking the answer using a calculator. If the players' answer is wrong, they miss a turn.

Copymasters 39 (Multiplication ladders) is a game for four players, using two pentagonal spinners (**resource copymaster R1**), one marked 1 to 5, the other 6 to 10. Each player has a 'tables' ladder, cut from a copy of copymaster 39. In turn, they spin one spinner of their choice, and enter the answer to the multiplication on their card that starts with the number on the spinner. The winner is the first player to complete their ladder. (Answers should be checked with a calculator.)

Area of study 29	P of S 3c	LD 3		

BEGINNING DIVISION

Commentary

Even before they are formally introduced to division, the children will have a concept of what it means in real life. The challenge for you is to introduce the ways for recording what 'sharing' does to numbers, without divorcing it from the idea of sharing toys with their sisters and brothers or cheese sandwiches with their mum. No matter how competent children are as mathematicians, do not be tempted to leave out the

practical work. Only links with real situations will convince many children that maths is relevant to them.

At Level 2, the children have met a half and a quarter. You may want to revise this work with them. The children will also have worked on multiplication. You will discover when it is appropriate to link multiplication and division. If the children have been given the confidence to play with numbers, some of them will find and point out the links themselves.

Activity 1: Playing 'sharing'

To play sharing, you and the children need access to a special resource box. Some of the things that might be found there are listed in Beginning multiplication, Activity 1, 'Playing "lots of"' above. Show the children that you can share play objects between a number of children or a number of toys. Avoid remainders at this stage.

Practise sharing out by, for example, sharing pencils between pencil cases, books into boxes and beads on to necklaces.

Let the children have many turns at sharing things out. Link their practical sharing to the moral dilemmas in sharing, and make up a little book of stories the children have written about what they share, at home and at school. Display the book in the maths or book corner, or use it as the basis for an assembly.

Activity 2: Picture 'sharing'

Let the children record in their books, the results of some picture 'sharing'. Set these out so that the children can join the shared item to the sharer.

Copymaster **40** (Picture sharing) presents some sample examples for the children to do.

Area of study	P of S	LD
30	**3c**	**3**

FIRST DIVISIONS

C37, 41–43

Commentary

Children who understand addition, subtraction and multiplication, will quickly be able to convert their practical 'sharing' activity, using each other and toys, to an activity they can set out on a table or in their books. Now is the time to give them the mathematical words and sign for division. But, once again, be careful about setting the method as the challenge rather than the concept of division.

Activity 1: Practical 'share by'

Using practical resources, let the children set out and talk you or their friends through some 'share by' examples. Give them problem cards, with all the items for counting on them. The children can then lay out the counting aids to match each card, and use the resources to find the answer.

Activity 2: 'Share by' language and sign

Use 'shared between', 'division', 'divided by', 'size of share' and the sign '÷' with the children and add them to the maths language book or class chart.

Activity 3: Division

The children will need to record the patterns in these problems. Before you give them random problems, let them see what happens to the size of share as the number to be shared increases, and work out how many shares there can be, of a given size, in a big number.

Copymaster **41** presents some division puzzles.
Copymaster **42** presents divide cards for the game of 'Zap! which is on **copymaster 37**.

Activity 4: Division and multiplication links

If the children do not see the links between division and multiplication, and remark on them, use things from the resource box to point out that, for example, $6 \div 2 = 3$ and $2 \times 3 = 6$.

Let the children convert some multiplications to divisions.

Activity 5: Division using the calculator

Let children mark, check and set divisions using calculators. Now is the time to give them questions involving all four operations, allowing them to check their answers on the calculator.

Copymasters **43** (Calculator checks) is a mixed bag of calculations suitable for checking with a calculator.

Activity 6: Remainders
Show the children that if you share 9 sweets between Dawn and Jenny they will have 4 each and there will be 1 left over. Tell the children that this is called the 'remainder'. Play practical sharing with remainders.

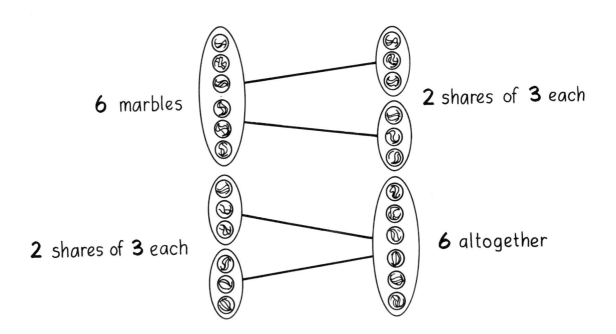

6 marbles

2 shares of 3 each

2 shares of 3 each

6 altogether

| Area of study 31 | P of S 3c | LD 3 | **MULTIPLICATION AND DIVISION FACTS** ▶ |

Commentary
We would see the approach to this Area of study as being through pattern making like that described in Areas of study 18, 19 and 20. When the children have a sense of the patterns in, for example, counting in twos, it is a small step to the two times table and a knowledge of 2× and ÷2 facts.

Activity 1: 2s, 5s and 10s
Practice these orally and in writing, using real objects, patterns, apparatus and calculators. Quick fire oral puzzles of the kind 'What are four fives?', 'How many tens in forty' and 'Count in twos from sixteen to twenty four', will help children to memorise these facts.

Colour patterns of 2s, 5s and 10s into a hundred square as in Area of study 20, activity 2, and look for products appearing in more than one pattern.

Activity 2: Testing, testing
Ask the children to set four or five multiply or division puzzles each. Compile a bank of these and let the class try one or two a day, either orally or in writing. Let them know who 'set the test' for the day, and if it is brief they will regard it as more 'fun' than a long formal effort set by the teacher. You can then add one or two questions on some days. For example: 'Write two numbers that are products in the pattern of ×3 and ×6.

Programme of study: Number

■ 3. Understanding relationships between numbers and developing methods of computation

Pupils should be taught to:

d develop a variety of methods for adding and subtracting, including using the fact that subtraction is the inverse of addition;

Area of study	P of S	LD
32	3d	3

VARIETY OF COMPUTATION STRATEGIES ▶

Commentary

The point to tackle here is that children, in the light of their understanding of addition and subtraction, will have a number of ways of viewing the calculations given them.

Here are a number of ways of talking about additions and subtractions which have implications for how they are viewed:

— taking away (how many are left?)
— inverse or complementary addition (What must we add to … to make …?)
— comparison (how much more is … than … ?)

Activity 1: Computation talk

In the light of the points made in the commentary discuss with the children a variety of ways of explaining what is happening when they tackle additions and subtractions. Here are some suggested situations to discuss: 10 apples on a tree and 3 fall to the ground; Simon spends 8p of his 20p pocket money; Simon gets 20p pocket money and his brother Liam gets 25p; Polly has 30 stickers and needs 8 more to have the same as Sue.

Programme of study: Number

■ **3. Understanding relationships between numbers and developing methods of computation**

Pupils should be taught to:

● use a basic calculator, reading the display, *eg use the constant function to explore repeated addition.*

Area of study	P of S	LD
33	3e	2

USING A CALCULATOR ▶

Commentary

The advent of cheap calculators means that we all have powerful computational power literally at our fingertips. Teachers and children worry that using calculators seems like cheating. However, we are in an electronic age and it would therefore be foolish to exclude the use of calculators in everyday school work. Their use does need to be matched with a concern to ensure that children can do those everyday, mental mathematical operations that human beings are capable of carrying out. As well as doing these and being able to use a calculator children need to have powers of estimation and prediction. These cannot be gleaned by using a calculator but only through practical application.

Calculators vary in their operation. When buying calculators try to ensure that they have, apart from the usual computational features, the following:

● a memory;
● iteration (You can test this by pressing a number, say 2, followed by '+' then '=' repeatedly. This should give a display which increments by two each time.);
● a clear display;
● 'solar' power.

Additional features are not mandatory. However, if children have scientific calculators of their own which have facilities such as automatic use of square roots, you may have to find out how to explain these features to the proud new owner!

The Activities in this section are related to all of the mathematics done at Level 4. Allow the children to make full use of calculators within the context of their need to understand processes and principles. The calculator should not become something to be learned, rather it is a tool for learning.

Activity 1: Looking at a calculator

Let the children look hard at the calculator keypad and ask them questions about it; for example 'Which number is above 5?' 'How many rows of keys are there?' Show the children how to put the calculator on and off, if it is not solar powered.

Activity 2: Calculator play

Let the children experiment by pressing keys at will and explaining what happens. Then ask them to do some simple tasks. For example they should try $2 + = , = , = , =$ and then additions like $1 + 2 + 3 =$. Ask them to put in the biggest number they can, and the smallest number. Then let them try adding register figures, dinner money totals and shopping lists.

Programme of study: Number

Pupils should be taught to:

■ 4. Solving numerical problems

a understand the operations of addition, subtraction as taking away and comparison, and the relationship between them, recognise situations to which they apply and use them to solve problems with whole numbers, including situations involving money;

b understand the operations of multiplication, and division as sharing and repeated subtraction, and use them to solve problems with whole numbers or money, understanding and dealing appropriately with remainders;

c choose a suitable method of computation, using apparatus where appropriate, or a calculator where the numbers include several digits;

d begin to check answers in different ways, *eg repeating the calculation in a different order or using a different method*, and gain a feel for the appropriate size of an answer.

> These points from the Programme of study have been placed together, for work in the Areas of study that follow can contribute to any or all of these points. For example, 'play' activities can be made complex and challenging, including division, remainders, numbers with several digits and opportunities to calculate in a variety of ways.

Area of study	P of S	LD
34	4a	1

NUMBERS IN PLAY

Commentary

The best arena for children to do real counting is provided by role play games in the classroom. There are many possible settings for this work. We suggest a few here and will develop these in Areas of study 35 and 41. Play counts like those below set the scene for problem solving at a later stage.

Activity 1: Play house

In the home corner, create a one-roomed house. It could be the house for the following:

● The three bears (counting, one-to-one correspondence, sequencing)
● Red Riding Hood's grandma (First Red Riding Hood says, 'My, what big ears . . .' etc., ordinal number)
● A 'real' family (number on house, knocks at the door, counting in the cupboard – numbers of cups, plates, etc.; setting the table – one-to-one correspondence; dressing the baby doll – ordinal number).

Activity 2: Play shop

The play house can become a shop, with a table inside, set against the open window as a counter. Fill the till or cash box with play coins and exchange single items for a coin. The children can count the items and count the coins. Try letting the children play with these:

● Play dough fruits or cakes (a recipe for this dough is in 'Resourcing your mathematics' at the beginning of the book)
● Paper hats
● Play lollipops
● Old greeting cards.

Theme play shops are suggested in Area of study 35.

Activity 3: Play post office

This kind of play shop has much potential. Try:

● Sticky labels with a picture drawn on them as stamps
● Old postcards and greeting cards
● Parcel string
● Gift tags.

Activity 4: Play telephone

A strong cardboard box like those used for dishwashers or cookers makes a good kiosk. When painted and decorated, set up an old phone or a play phone in it. Put in a box with a slot for coins, and a list of important phone numbers.

● How many bandages are needed for two arms and two legs (counting/addition)?
● Teddy Growl is going home, how many patients will be left (practical subtraction)?

Activity 6: Play spaceship

This needs more setting up than the others, though an upended table with a sheet over it and cone of silver foil covered card on top will do. Supply the astronauts with helmets – large cereal packets with holes cut for the face and foil covering are adequate. Also supply the following:

● A flight log to fill in (counting and sequencing)
● A countdown chart
● A picture route map (sequencing).

Activity 5: Play hospital

Create a doctor's bag with equipment. Let the children set out the 'ward' of beds (boxes) with toys or child patients and solve problems like:

● How many beds do six patients need (one-to-one correspondence)?
● If two patients came in today and there were three already, how many altogether (practical addition)?

Area of study 35	P of S 4a	LD 2	**NUMBER PLAY AT LEVEL 2**

Commentary

The arena for giving the children number 'problems' should be an active practical situation. For example, sums about pocket money are more fun when you have play money and piggy banks. 'Problems' sorted out in a practical way are more like maths in real life. Create role play situations in which the children can do work on estimation, number bonds to ten, counting and halves and quarters. The possible range of situations is endless. We have chosen a few, and extended the work begun at Level 1 in these settings.

Activity 1: Play house

Use and extend the house set up for Level 1 work. For example:

● Hang a picture with numbers of things in it on the play house wall
● Put a number of teddies and a number of dolls in the house
● Set the table with a number of places, and a matching (or not quite matching) number of chairs
● Put pans on the 'cooker'
● Put play fruit in the bowl

● Put shopping in the shopping basket.

You can then confine the use of the play house to a group of children doing this number work through the day.

Then set problems, including things like:
● How many teddies are at home today? How many dolls? How many toys altogether?

The play house is a maths workshop

51

● How many trees in the picture? How many flowers? How many trees and flowers?
● How many people are going to have lunch?
● If yellow Ted eats two apples from the bowl, how many fruits will be left?
● If the things in the shopping basket cost 2p each, how much was spent on shopping?

Activity 2: Play shop

Extending the shop ideas you used at Level 1, you can begin to give the things prices up to 10p and ask the children to take a shopping list and buy and total their items. They can also do quite complex puzzles. If you have a 'corner shop' or little supermarket, they can try things like:

● Is the pop more expensive than the juice?
● Which is the cheapest pack of biscuits?
● Are Crunchflakes cheaper than Crummos?
● What can you buy for 10p?

● How much do six eggs cost?
● What is the best teatime bargain in the shop?
● If you have 10p to spend, and use only 8p, how much change will there be?

Or create a shop with a theme. Here are some ideas:

● Seaside shop, carrying sand toys, flags, pretend rock, correctly named seashells, postcards
● Gloves, handbags, scarves and hats
● Garden centre, stocking trowels, dibbers, flower pots, pretend packets of seeds, gardening gloves and pot plants (which could be real or models)
● Fruit and vegetables
● Stationery, cards and gifts
● Jewelry, including homemade badges, beads, wristwatches and clocks
● Birthdays, including cards, serviettes, paper cups, party bags, party hats and pretend cakes
● Christmas, including decorations, things for a tree, tags and cards

Activity 3: Play hospital

The hospital can become a health clinic, and the 'doctor' can estimate, record and count how many patients she has seen in a week. You can supply some invented records for the children to add to. Or you could recruit a play dentist to count, for example:

● The number of teeth
● Wiggly teeth
● How many teeth the patients have lost.

Charts and wall posters can help. There are lots of measures and potential for health education here.

Activity 4: Play post office

At the post office, the children can learn about savings, licences, allowances, and buy little books of stamps. You can wrap parcels of predetermined weights and they can work out what the postage is. The post office can stock things of varying prices including pencils, rubbers and pens; party invitations, serviettes and paper cups; envelopes and writing paper.

Activity 6: Play telephone

Extend the work done in the play telephone box by pricing each call and asking the children to add up their calls. You can vary the price of calls by saying that calls to people inside the building are 10p and outside (just outside the building) are 20p. You can give a scale of prices for calls according to when they are made: attach a notice in the box to say that morning calls are 20p and afternoon calls half price.

It may be sensible to discuss with the children the real cost of phone calls!

Activity 7: Play spaceship
List the planets in the solar system. Ask the children to decide where they are going and in what order. Make up ideas for space meals.

   SOLVING NUMBER MYSTERIES

Area of study	P of S	LD
36	4a	2

C44

Commentary
Tell the children that mathematicians often use a letter of the alphabet to indicate missing information. The idea of finding this information from a set of clues underpins the solution of algebraic equations.

Activity 1: Maths mysteries using children
Explain to the children that mathematicians are often

trying to find out what a mystery number is. Show the children a practical problem, using the children themselves as the resource, and work through it with them to demonstrate the idea that assembling all you know may enable you to find what is missing. Below is an example.

Try out some more problems using the children as a resource.

3   +   ?   =   5

Activity 2: Maths mysteries using apparatus

Use counting aids and other equipment to create more 'missing number mysteries'. You could create a cardboard 'maths detective', or dress the class teddy in suitable clothes to identify the kinds of mysteries you are working on.

Create a display of number mysteries you have solved with the children, and set a new one out each day, that they can try when they have a moment to spare. Then at the end of each day work through it, or better still, ask one of the children who has solved it to explain how they did it. The problem can be added to a class dossier, which can go in the reading corner after the display is taken down.

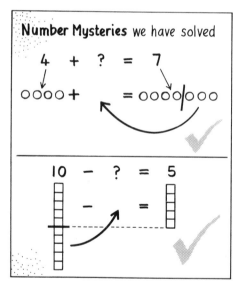

Activity 3: What is the mystery number?

The problems can now be set out using conventional notation. Let the children use counting aids to work out the answers, but try not to let them lose the idea that it is a bit of detective work, as in Activities 1 and 2 above. When you mark their work, you can let the children know how many mysteries they have solved, that these cases are closed, and so on. Remember to give the children as wide a variety of layouts as possible. Here are some examples:

$$2 + 3 = ?$$
$$5 + ? = 6$$
$$? + 7 = 9$$
$$\Box + 5 = 10$$
$$3 + \Box = 4$$
$$7 = \Box + 2$$
$$10 = 2 + \Box$$

Copymaster 44 supplies some missing number mysteries.

Area of study 37	P of S 4ab	LD 2	**PLAY AT MATHS DETECTIVE**	C45 –47

Commentary

This final section presents some ideas for giving the children some independence in trying to solve problems.

One of the major difficulties in mathematics teaching is the general impression that mathematics is about finding one (right) solution. The preoccupation of many children, and adults, is getting the answer right. While it is important to be accurate and, where appropriate, provide the correct outcome of a computation, it is equally important that children come to see mathematics as exploratory and problems as being amenable to different approaches and solutions.

Activity 1: Robots

As an introduction to function machines place a big cardboard box on the floor. Cut two slots in it, one at each end. Let a child get into the box. Other children can post a numeral into one slot. The child in the box takes it and posts another numeral out of the other end. The children looking on have to decide what the 'function machine' has done to the number. You, as teacher, can record the operation of the function machine.

Let the children create their own robots using cartons and silver foil. They can set each other robot mysteries, by placing the 'secret' in the robot's tummy, and then showing their partner what number goes into one ear and what number comes out of the other! Make a display of the robots.

Copymasters 45 (An add 3 robot) and **46** (A take away 2 machine) present the children with some robot calculations.

Activity 3: Laying a number trail

Let the children work in small groups to develop a missing number trail. They will need to draw up the prototype on a large sheet of paper, and then let you check it before laying a trail which some of their classmates can try the following day.

What happens here?

Activity 2: Follow the number trail

Set a number trail in the classroom, where the children have to find out a mystery number at every stage. Let the children do this independently, when they have a few minutes, and record their final answer on a secrets chart (which can have anonymous entries). At the end of the day check through the trail with the children.

There is a number mini-trail on **copymaster 47** (Computation trail).

| Area of study 38 | P of S 4a | LD 2 | **SOLVING PROBLEMS AND 'FINDING THE DIFFERENCE'** | C48 |

Commentary

If you give the children the sums $6 + 3$ and $3 + 6$, they may do them independently and not make connections between them. Children get used to the idea of 'one sum at a time', and then fail to recognise that addition is commutative, that is:

$$6 + 3 = 3 + 6$$

Once they know this, they will commonly begin to tackle addition by taking the bigger number first, no matter how the sum is presented. They will do $2 + 8$ as though it were $8 + 2$, because it seems easier *and* gives the same answer.

As well as getting to grips with commutativity, children also need to understand the associativity of addition. For example, they need to understand that

$$(3 + 6) + 4 = 3 + (6 + 4)$$

and that the right-hand version is a lot easier to handle in this particular example!

While addition is commutative, subtraction is not.

$$6 - 3 \neq 3 - 6 \quad (\neq \text{ means does not equal})$$

Nor is subtraction associative.

$$(9 - 6) - 3 \neq 9 - (6 - 3)$$

Children need both to understand commutativity and associativity, and to know where each is applicable.

Play situations at this level are ideal arenas to develop children's computation skills in practical problem-solving situations.

Activity: Mix and match

Give the children additions and subtractions in mixed exercises. Discuss the configurations of numbers, the ways of tackling calculations by, for example, starting with the larger number in additions and the larger number in subtractions (which can be done no other way at this stage).

A single sample page of these problems is presented on **copymaster 48** (Add and subtract).

The children should now be ready to tackle number problems like those that can be presented in the class shop, or other play situations. Look, for example, at 'Number play at Level 2', Activity 2.

Area of study	P of S	LD
39	4ac	2

SHOPPING

C49, 50

Commentary

Shopping is familiar to every child. However, that does not necessarily mean they understand how the system works. We have a suggested discussion list here, which should take the children from the idea of 'swopping' to an understanding of equivalence.

Activity 1: Swopping

Investigate things known to have been used in barter, and let the children act out explorers swopping beads for rubber, fruit, and other exotic things. Pirates could swop new masts or flags for jewels. Create a barter system especially for the class, where yogurt pots, stickers or conkers become sought after, and the medium of exchange.

We still barter with one another. Discuss with the children the idea that we might give our neighbours some of our pears, and hope for some apples from the neighbour's tree in return.

Activity 2: Spending

Use a classroom shop (as discussed in 'Number play at Level 2') and shopping games, to enable the children to practise spending money. Begin with 1p coins, and gradually introduce others.

There is a page of money equivalence problems on **copymaster 49** (Equivalence).

Activity 3: Change

When children understand equivalence and are adept at simple mental addition and subtraction they will be able to begin working on giving change. Let them try it in the classroom shop, and on paper.

Copymaster 50 (Change) has some shopping problems.

Activity 4: Bills

In the classroom shop (or restaurant, see 'Number play at Level 2') the children can begin to write down a list of items, add up the total cost, and then check their answers on the calculator.

Area of study	P of S	LD
40	4ab	3

FUNCTION MACHINES

C51 –54

Commentary

In work in Level 2 algebra the children met 'number robots'. This work is a continuation.

The use of function machines can fire children's motivation and allows them the chance to create their own machines. This reinforces a problem-solving and investigative approach to mathematics. It also provides children with a set of experiences which will open up work on graphs and relationships at a later stage.

Activity 1: Working function machines

Cut a piece out of either end of a small box (a box which once held tea bags, packet soup or cornflour is ideal) so that the box looks like a bridge. Mark one hole 'IN' and the other 'OUT'.

Place a piece of card under the box with, for example, '+2' on it. Now post a piece of card in the 'IN' side, with a numeral, for example 1, on it. Ask the children: 'If this was a machine and we posted in 1 and inside there was +2, what would we expect to come out?' When the children call out '3', place a piece of card with the numeral 3 on it near the 'OUT' hole.

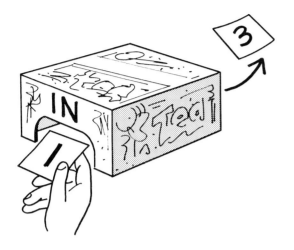

Try this again, leaving the +2 card inside, and pushing in other numbers. The children will soon see that the 'machine' is a 'calculation machine'. Try changing the card inside, and try subtraction as well as addition cards. Tell the children that this is a function machine, and the function is what is happening to the number put in to get the number that comes out.

Copymasters 51 (An add 5 rocket), **52** (A take away 7 machine) and **53** (Star wars machines) give the children a chance to work out the outputs of function machines.

Activity 2: Finding the function

Try Activity 1 again, putting a mystery function inside the 'machine'. With the clues of some inputs and outputs the children should be able to determine what the function is.

Copymaster 54 (Mystery machines) presents some machines, and the children can find out what they might do.

Activity 3: Inventing function machines

Let the children make their own function machines from boxes or cartons and play at giving each other problems of these sorts:

● 'Here is what is in the machine, here is the number in, what is the number out?'

● (Put a function unseen into machine.) 'Here is the number in and the number out. What is the machine doing?'

● 'Keeping the same number in, what can we do to change the number out?'

● 'Keeping the same number out, what can we do to change the number in?'

Area of study	P of S	LD
41	4abc	3

PLAY AT LEVEL 3

Commentary

Some teachers seem to feel that active play with number is the prerogative of the reception class. Our view is that, in all areas of learning, we are too quick to move away from real situations and first-hand experience to the abstract and information at second hand. We are not suggesting that 'exploratory' role play should be continued (except for the children who need it) beyond the first few terms of schooling. However, 'number play' situations continue to be appropriate throughout all the classes in the primary school. At Level 3, you will see that we have extended what is expected in those same play situations that we worked on at Level 2. We have focused the situations a little more. The tasks set are carefully specified, and the 'play' situation need only be set up for the time it takes for the appropriate children to do the work. If your working space, ingenuity and time permit, it would be possible to create, for example, a play post office, where all the children have a go at doing the tasks appropriate for each of them, whether they are working at Level 1, 2 or 3.

Activity 1: Play house

Give the children a series of problems to do, using the play house as their starting point. For example:

● Give the house a number, and ask the children which house numbers would appear on either side (odds and evens).

● Create an inventory of contents, and ask the children to check it out, including things like: 'How many items are in the cupboard? or 'How much money is in the purse?' (numbers to 20 and beyond).

● Create a calendar for the house, including birthdays and social events for the toys (computation and time).

● Make a play TV from a box and make up a *TV Times* of children's programmes (programme length and viewing hours).

● Write a menu for play house meals (counting, weighing, recipes, cooking times and temperatures, sequencing, health education).

● Write a shopping list to link with the menu (money, estimation, approximation).

● Start a database using the play house as the prototype, and include how many rooms, doors, windows and similar information. The children can collect the same information for their own or their classmates' homes, to add to the database.

Activity 2: Play shop

Set up a supermarket or theme shop, like those listed in 'Play shop' (page 35) at Level 2.

You could even set up a shop to serve both maths and English. One example is a 'story' shop, which is really a bank of resources that the children can use for story writing. The appeal is that it is flexible, for you can change the 'stock' and the children can choose what they 'buy' for their story. For example, with a spending limit of £1, or four items, Roxanne assembled for her story the following things:

model castle	60p
paper flag	2p
princess doll	30p
cardboard bridge	8p

She could begin her story with the tale of her 'magic' shopping trip, or the shopping could be part of maths and the story begins 'Once upon a time . . .'

On another day Asif might collect from the shop the following:

a 'giant' sock and a little one total	50p
a large model cake	15p
a bag labelled 'magic dust'	32p

What a book of stories a group of children can produce! And each will be different.

Challenge the children when they are 'shopping' by asking them to create shopping lists, work out change, look for 'bargains' and take advantage of sales and special offers. If, for example, the children complete a shopping expedition one day, and the following day everything is half price, they can see what happens to the shopping bill. They can also work out the cost of multiples of one item costing say 8p or 10p and find the number of things at, for example, 2p each, that they can buy for a given amount.

Activity 3: Play post office

Extend the children's experience at Levels 1 and 2 by, for example, doing some of the following activities:

● Introduce the children to the course a real letter takes when it is posted, and role play the journey of a letter

● Look at the actual postal rates for letters and parcels, and create some letters and packets that can be weighed and the postage determined

● Make a study of addresses and postcodes, looking at patterns of numbering and what postcodes mean.

Activity 4: Play telephone

Extension activities, beyond the experience gained at Levels 1 and 2, could include the following:

● Play remembering number sequences and help the children to memorise their home telephone numbers

● Make the calls have a purpose now, and play 'fax' with messages they have typed on a typewriter or word processor

● Use the telephone book to set problem numbers to look up.

Activity 5: Play spaceship

Some more challenging activities here include:

● Let the children find out all they can about a recent space probe and record the numerical data.

● Draw their own race or maze game, using numbers and space as a theme.

● Find out earth information about time across the world.

| Area of study 42 | P of S 4c | LD 3 | **CHOOSING COMPUTATION METHODS** | C55, 56 |

Commentary
If children have had a wide experience of circumstances in which to use addition, subtraction, multiplication and division, they should be confident enough to be able to identify new situations in which these operations are appropriate. This section will also enable you to establish who needs more help in order to be confident.

Activity 1: Which operation?
Give the children a variety of problems and ask them to do their work in two steps. Firstly they should say whether they are going to use addition, subtraction, multiplication or division. Secondly they can carry through the calculation.

Sample problems appear on **copymaster 55** for the children to complete. **Copymaster 56** employs larger numbers, and children may find the use of a calculator necessary.

| Area of study 43 | P of S 4d | LD 3 | **CHECKING ANSWERS** | C57, 58 |

Commentary
This work is linked to a thorough understanding of place value. Knowing the appropriate size of an answer is all the more important in everyday life now that we use electronic cash machines in supermarkets, and calculators and digital displays.

Activity 1: Just checking
Using some calculations the children have already done, ask them to check their answers and demonstrate how they checked them. For example, if they had done a calculation like this: $18 + 19 = 37$, they could then try $20 + (18 - 1)$, $19 + 18$, $20 + 20 - 2 - 1$, $37 - 18 = 19$, and so on.

Copymasters 57 and **58** offer checking opportunities.

| Area of study 44 | P of S 4d | LD 3 | **MENTAL COMPUTING MADE EASIER** | C57 –59 |

Commentary
Give the children opportunities to break two-digit numbers into smaller numbers in order to make computation easier. For example, if 43 becomes $40 + 3$, it may be easier to manipulate when adding another number to it.

The children should also be confident with approximation as a device for helping with calculations. If we know that 99 is very nearly 100, we can do a calculation with 99 in it as though it were 100, and make a deduction of 1 at the end to give the accurate answer.

Activity 1: Breaking down numbers
Practise breaking down numbers into tens and units, before doing complex additions and subtractions with a group of children. Work through some calculations as a group, then let the children do some individual recording.

There are calculations with space for breaking the numbers into tens and units on **copymasters 57** (Tens and units: addition) and **58** (Tens and units: subtraction).

Activity 2: Rough then right
Play approximations with the children. For example, they should be able to say that 28 is nearly 30 and 51 is

close to 50. When they can do this unerringly, show them how this knowledge can be applied in calculations. Try working some through with the children and then let them work in pairs, and finally individually. At the end of each session, each child can choose a calculation and explain how they did it. A message from you at the bottom of their work, about the way they delivered their explanations, will help their confidence and their work in Using and applying mathematics.

Copymaster 59 presents some calculations where approximation steps can be entered in.

Activity 3: All in the head
When the children are confident with the processes in Activities 1 and 2, they can try doing similar calculations in their heads. To have evidence of mental work you will need to ban counting aids, and ask the children to show you their answers. The children may find it helpful to use a two-stage operation, where they write their answers on the left-hand page in their book, get them marked, and then write down the steps they went through in their heads on the right-hand page.

Programme of study: Number

Pupils should be taught to:

■ **5. Classifying, representing and interpreting data**

a sort and classify a set of objects using criteria related to their properties, *eg size, shape, mass*;

Area of study 45	P of S 5a

SORTING

Commentary

Many children will be familiar with sorting before they come to school. If parents have let them sort the washing into whites and coloureds, the shoes into pairs or the shopping from the basket, they will be able to put things together, and say what is the same about them.

The focus in the activities below is on developing the children's strategies for choosing criteria for sorting.

Begin with a single criterion for sorting – for example, aged 6/not aged 6 – and later introduce two or three sorts which may overlap.

Activity 1: Beginning sorting

If the children have already done work in other sections of this book, they will have had practice in sorting in school. If you are starting them here, begin with the children themselves. Sort a group out according to whether, for example, they are boys or girls, they have blonde hair or not, they have long or short socks. At first you may need to tell the children how you have made the sort. Soon they will be able to guess.

Let them take turns at sorting out the rest of the group while the group members guess the basis of the sort.

Activity 2: Sorting children's belongings

Having used the children themselves in Activity 1 you can now turn to the next resource to the children themselves, namely their possessions. Play at sorting hats and coats, shoe bags and pencil cases, plimsolls and lunch boxes.

Let the children do some sorting of these and guess the criteria for each other's sorts.

Activity 3: Sorts using pictures

Let the children use a selection of toys and equipment from the classroom or pictures from magazines. If the pictures are mounted on card and laminated they will remain usable for several groups of children. As with the sorts in Activities 1 and 2, begin by doing some yourself and letting the children guess the basis of the sort. Then let them sort for each other. When not in use these things can be laid out on a table, so that the children can handle and sort them themselves.

Our Sorting table

STORIES

Sort the toys into sets

Activity 4: About children

Use information about the children to put them into sets. Here are some suggestions:

- Those who have/have not a pet cat
- Those who have/have not a brother
- Those who live/do not live in a flat
- Those whose house has/has not a back garden.

You can also make two- or three-way sorts, depending on the size of the group of children. For example:

- Live in a flat/bungalow/house
- Have/have not a brother/have more than one brother.

This information makes excellent material for you to put in a class book which can be added to the maths resources. Though the children should not be made to record their sorts you could use pictures of 'Heather's cat' and 'Kelvin's house' to illustrate the book.

Activity 5: How many ways can you sort?

Show the children a small number of items for sorting, about six in all. The challenge is, without moving them at all, they should think of as many ways of sorting them as possible. You can then ask a child to show all the sorts, and then add the other children's new ideas. This activity will give you a way of assessing whether the children have mastered the concept of sorting.

CHOOSE CRITERIA, SORT AND RECORD

Area of study 46 | P of S 5a | R8–11

Commentary

Following on from the opportunities that you will already have given to children to sort on limited criteria, provided by you, we are now at the stage where the children need to be able to start offering their own criteria.

As well as taking responsibility for sorting, the children should also be making decisions about how to record. Their repertoire of recording approaches can be extended.

Activity 1: Guess my sort

If the children have had much practice at sorting at Level 1, they should now be able to carry through a sort of their own devising, from the initial stage of assembling the collection of objects or deciding the categories of data, through to recording the outcomes. As a preliminary to this process, let them take turns at doing sorts and see if their friends can guess the basis for the sort. They can do this in classtime, while you look on or visit the group every few minutes, or you can set up a sorting table and allow each child to assemble a number of sorts each day, leaving them on display. Others in their group can predict the bases for these sorts and put their ideas into a suggestion box. You can then gather the group together to discuss the sorts each day.

Activity 2: Recording results of sorts

The children can devise their own ways of recording the sorts that they do. When they have developed a range of ways, you can show them any which they may not have thought of, including, for example, the following:

- Venn, Carroll or tree diagrams (see page 108)
- String and collage
- Folding or partitioning paper
- Charts.

Resource copymasters R8 (Venn diagram: two discrete sets) and **R9** (Sets: four discrete) present blanks recording sorts of discrete sets. Use **resource copymasters R10** (Venn diagram: two overlapping sets) and **R11** (Carroll diagram) for more complex sorts.

Programme of study: Number

■ **5. Classifying, representing and interpreting data**

Pupils should be taught to:

b collect, record and interpret data arising from an area of interest, using an increasing range of charts, diagrams, tables and graphs.

Area of study 47	P of S 5b

FIRST RECORDING

Commentary

Several times in this book we have asked that the children should not be expected to record too soon. When handling data, in order to collect and organise it, the children will need to record, if only to support their memories. They should still have plenty of sorting without recording before committing anything to paper.

Activity 1: Concrete records

Let the children assemble and order data about themselves and things around them by physically using the children and the equipment. For example, if a child has made a sort of his/her work group into those wearing/not wearing red, he/she can physically line up the 'red wearers' apart from the 'not red wearers'. The range of data available about the children and equipment in the room is remarkably wide, but here are some possible starter suggestions:

● *The children themselves*
  – Aspects of clothing
  – Hairstyles and length
  – Eye colour
  – Foot or shoe size.
● *The children's belongings*
  – Colours/sizes of shoe bag
  – Styles of schoolbag
  – Size of plimsolls
  – Break-time snacks (using the wrappers as the data).
● *Classroom equipment*
  – Sets of shapes
  – Pencils according to size/colour
  – Soft toys
  – Crayons or chalks.

Activity 2: Freehand drawing

The first step in recording data on paper is by drawing.

At first let the children record on plain paper, without attempting to organise their recording for them. The sources of data are numerous, and you can also use pictures the children have drawn in other contexts. If, for example, Anthea has drawn herself and her dog, this is a recording of data about herself and demonstrates one-to-one correspondence. When Fred draws the class goldfish, he may not only record the set of goldfish, but also the number of goldfish and some data about their habitat. Of course the drawings children do in relation to sets in maths are relevant here.

Activity 3: Colouring in

When the children have drawn information about the data they are working with, you may like to introduce colouring as a recording activity. If you supply a picture of a train and ask Mandy to colour the first carriage blue, by colouring appropriately she is recording data. In a picture with several shapes, you can ask Hussein to colour just the triangles. Hussein then represents the number of and characteristics of triangles by 'tagging' them with a colour. Many commercially produced maths schemes rely on this kind of recording.

Hussein coloured the triangles

Mandy coloured the first truck blue

These colourings give us information. Can you find the **triangles**... ...and the **first truck** ?

Activity 4: Using templates

Let children use templates to record information. Giving children templates can help to reduce the number of skills they bring to bear on a task, and make the outcome more to their satisfaction. These can include shapes to draw round, shapes to stick on and shapes to print. For example:

● Melanie can draw round a rectangle to represent the number of windows in the classroom
● Mick can stick on circles to show the ladybirds on the school rose bush
● Tina can print a potato cut for every girl in the class.

Ladybirds on a bush — Mick

Melanie

Windows in the classroom

Girls in our class — Tina

| Area of study 48 | P of S 5b | MAPPING | C60, 61 |

Commentary

The idea of correspondence and, in particular, one-to-one correspondence (whether of one thing or one group of things) is an important concept. 'Mapping' like this lies at the root of being able to build the notion of functions in mathematics and the portrayal of relationships through graphical representation.

Activity 1: Concrete one-to-one correspondence

Let the children use each other as their first resource. They can, for example:

● match boy to girl to make 'pairs'
● match shoe bag or coat to child
● match lunch box or snack to child

If you have a play house the children can also use the toys from that to demonstrate one-to-one correspondence. For example:

● Bowls, chairs and beds for teddies
● Pram, cover, rattle for dolly.

Big Ted   Midi Ted   Baby Ted

Big Ted's bowl   Midi Ted's bowl   Baby Ted's bowl

Activity 2: Mapping one-to-one

When the children are ready to record their concrete mapping activities, you can let them draw, for example, the three bears, each with a bowl, or themselves with their pet or a pencil or book each. You can then give the children mapping exercises to do, using pictures.

There are some starter ideas on **copymaster 60** (Mapping).

Activity 3: Talk about mapping

The idea behind one-to-one correspondence is familiar to children in everyday life. However, they need not only to be able to do it, but also to be able to talk about what they are doing. Let the children tell each other of their mapping activities as they do them, and present what they have done with an oral explanation.

Activity 4: Complex mapping

One-to-one correspondence is the most familiar form of mapping. When the children are confident about doing this and articulate in talking about it, they will be able to handle more complex mapping. Try some of these examples:

- Teacher to children (one-to-many)
- Families – children to parents or kittens to cats (many-to-many)
- Coloured pencils to child (many-to-one).

There are some examples on **copymaster 61** (Complex mapping).

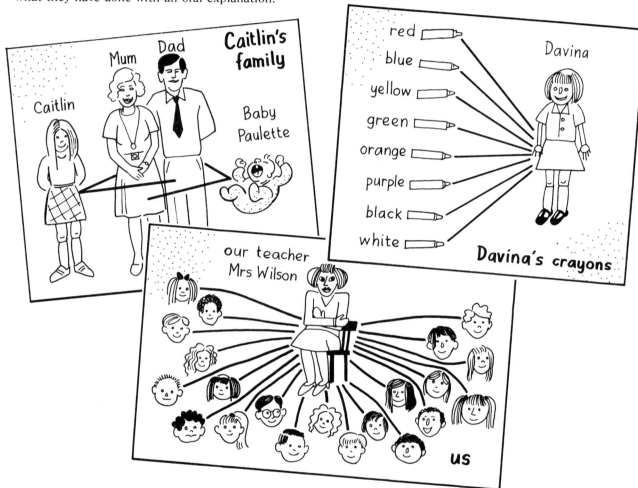

Area of study	P of S
49	5b

FREQUENCY TABLES

C62 –64

Commentary

The kind of data you choose for frequency table work depends on the location of the school and classroom and the number of children in the group. If the data has to be collected spasmodically you want to avoid the children wasting time waiting, when nothing is happening; you also want a fair rate of data input to maintain the children's motivation. Thus, predicted occurrence should be your guide to deciding what information to collect.

We have included the design of data collection sheets as a separate activity, because the children need to have mastered all the necessary research skills to data collection and presentation in order to understand the problems in research design.

Activity 1: Putting information in order
Discuss with the children the reasons why we put information in order, on charts and so on. Show the children things which demonstrate information put in order. Make a display to which they can bring things to add. Here are some starter examples:

- Lists including
  – the register
  – a shopping list

  – a supermarket receipt
  – a library index
  – a book index.

- Tables including
  – the ingredients in foodstuffs (from packaging)
  – a train timetable
  – washing powder user instructions
  – postage required for weights of letters.

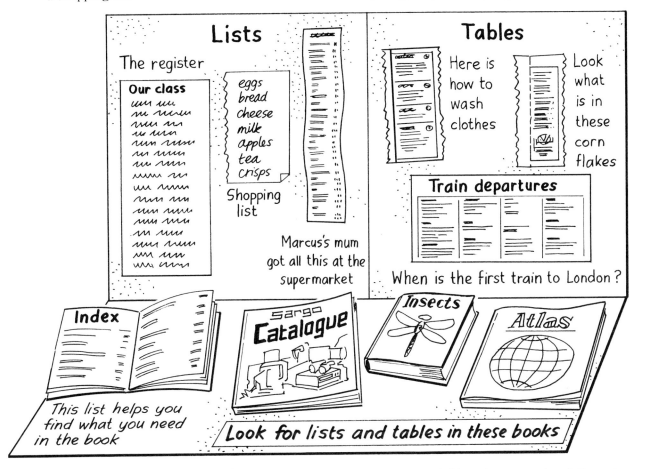

Note that the children do not need to fully understand how to interpret all these data sources at this Level – work at Level 3 supports this. You can also produce some data which has not been ordered and show the children how difficult it is to interpret.

Point out to the children that there are lots of ways of presenting information, and that we try to choose a way of setting it out that is easy to understand and gives ready access to the kind of information we will be needing. For example, if we repeatedly needed to work out which children lived closest to school, and then those that lived a little further away, and so on, teachers would keep a list of children, not alphabetical in terms of name, but perhaps by street name, starting with that closest to school.

Activity 2: How often?
The sources for the kind of information that children can easily transfer to a frequency table are legion. You could, for example, look at one of the following:

- Number of children in which class who pass your classroom door

Mrs Muddle's shopping list

Mrs Muddle's shopping
Can you see what she forgot to buy?

● Number of aircraft flying over the school in the morning/afternoon
● Number of times a few common words like 'the', 'and' and 'is' appear in a short book
● Number of sunny days in a month.

Because the children cannot create a frequency table before they can interpret one, it may be a good idea to let them work on some ready-made data first.

There are some imaginary data and a frequency chart on **copymaster 62** (Weather frequency table) which the children can discuss. **Copymaster 63** (Frequency data collection) is a suggested layout for the collection of data for a frequency chart. This could be added to a child's work file, when complete.

Activity 3: Designing data collection sheets
Suggest an experiment in data collection that the children may try. It may be one of those mentioned in Activity 2, or it may be, for example, the number of times the classroom door is opened in the first hour of schooling, every day for a week, or the number of times the school hamster uses its playwheel during each school day for a week. Ask the children what kinds of information they need to collect and for suggestions as to ways it could be laid out. If they suggest more than

one way, they could share out the ways of collecting information and try them. The outcomes of the work can be displayed.

Activity 4: Interpreting frequency charts
The children will need an understanding of how to interpret frequency charts in order to create and design them. The data children have collected can be added to a class resource bank and then used again by subsequent sets of children. You may ask successive sets of children to collect the same kind of data, so that you have some longitudinal indication of, for example, the number of aircraft that fly overhead, disturbing lesson time, or the number of times each of a range of books are read. If you have computer software enabling the creation of a database, this is just the kind of information which will be of interest, not only to you and the current set of children you teach, but subsequent sets of children and others working in the school.

Copymaster 64 (Customer frequency table) presents some imaginary data on a frequency table of people visiting various shops in a precinct, which you can use to demonstrate how the data can be interpreted, or which the children can write about. This is only an example, and not intended to replace first-hand data that children collect themselves.

 Area of study **50** | P of S **5b** ## BLOCK GRAPHS C65,66 R4,5

Commentary
The characteristics of block graphs are that:

● each column is discrete

● the blocks are all visually clear

● each column has its own label

● they allow a mix of numbers on one axis and labels on the other.

Activity 1: Concrete block graphs
Dividers from wine boxes, or pieces of card that have been interlocked can be very useful here, for these form a ready-made grid which will support things. Prop the grid against a backing sheet on which you have stuck or drawn numerals.

For small collections this structure can then be used to show how many toys of each kind are in a set, how many marbles of each colour in a bag, how many of each kind of shell, and so on.

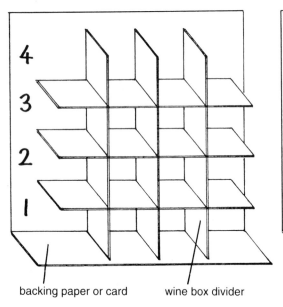

backing paper or card   wine box divider

bears | house | dolls | cars

Activity 2: Representative block graphs

The next best thing to being able to put a real object into the block graph is a representation of it. For example, if the children draw themselves, these pictures can be stuck onto block graph charts. These charts may show: months of birthdays, colour of eyes or hair, shoe size, age.

You can choose a symbol to place on the block graph which is self-explanatory. Here are some examples:

● Pictures of fruit to show favourite fruit
● Decorated matchboxes with tiny dolls peeping out to show bedtimes
● A design in colour to show favourite colours.

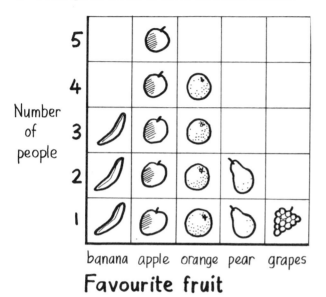

Favourite fruit

Activity 3: Using squared paper

Once the children have made concrete block graphs and representative block graphs they may find it straightforward to represent information on squared paper. You will need to mark in the axes for them, and work with them in counting the squares for each entry. They can then colour these in. You will know by your subsequent questioning whether they have a good understanding of what the squares of colour represent.

Resource copymasters **R4** and **R5** are for squared paper and **copymaster 65** is squared with axes drawn in. This may be appropriate for the block graphs the children do, depending on the numbers of items involved.

Activity 4: What goes on the axes?

For the children's first work on block graphs you will probably have decided on what goes along the axes and written it in. Try giving the children the opportunity of deciding how the information should be presented. If they come up with more than one suggestion, work through them with the children and see what the resulting graph looks like. The children should begin to make judgements about which presentation is clearer to them.

Activity 5: Assembling all the data

The next step is to let the children assemble the data they need for a block graph. Supply the children, working in pairs, with rough paper and a 'problem card'. It may say: 'Find out how many people's dads have moustaches, beards or are cleanshaven' or 'Test out which people in the class have ever eaten lychees, pomegranates, grapefruit and dates.' When they have collected the information ask them key questions like: 'How do you know you have asked everybody?' and 'How did you record people's answers?'

There are a number of problems set out on **copymaster 66**, which should be photocopied onto card, cut out and covered with protective film. These are examples of what the children may do, to which you can add suggestions related to the specific children with whom you are working.

Activity 6: Block graphs from start to finish

If the children have had practice in activities 1–5, they should now be able to have a go at collecting their own data and completing a block graph.

Remember there are axes drawn on squared paper on **copymaster 65**.

CARROLL, VENN AND TREE DIAGRAMS

Area of study 51 | P of S 5b | R8 –11

Commentary

Classifying objects on the basis of two different criteria permits the use of a simple diagram for displaying the data. This offers opportunities for the future in that many simple classification keys are based on such distinctions, and the use of diagrams in mathematics is an important development of some mathematical ideas.

Activity 1: 'Concrete' Carroll diagram

Let the children sort a collection of objects, and then sort again within those sets. They will then have two

sets, each made up of two subsets. For example, if you give the children a collection of shapes, including triangles, squares and circles that are red, yellow or blue, they could sort them into circles/not circles and then red/not red.

If you then give the children a piece of paper which is divided into four quarters, they can place each subset of the shapes on one area of the paper. You can mark the sections 'circles'/'not circles' and 'red'/'not red'.

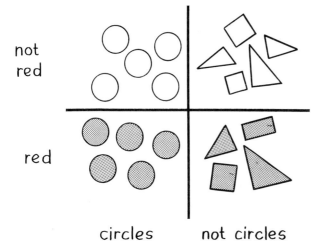

not
red

red

circles   not circles

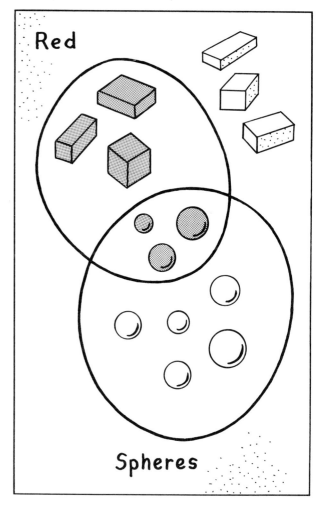

Red

Spheres

Activity 2: Recording a Carroll diagram

Let the children try to do some sorts themselves and place them on a sectioned piece of paper like that used in Activity 1. On another piece of paper they can record what they have sorted and the criteria for the sort.

Resource copymaster **R11** provides a grid suitable for Carroll diagrams.

Activity 3: 'Concrete' Venn diagram

Give the children a collection of objects which have been pre-selected by you to offer sorts according to two criteria. For example, you may give them red and blue beads that are spherical and cuboid.

Ask them to sort them out. They may choose red/not red. If they then sort by sphere/not sphere, they will have overlapping sets comprising 'red spheres', 'red not-spheres', 'not-red spheres', 'not-red not-spheres'. Let the children do a variety of sorts over a number of sessions.

Activity 4: Recording a Venn diagram

After plenty of practical sorts, the children can begin to record the results of their sorts on paper.

Resource copymasters **R8** and **R9** are suitable for recording sorts of discrete sets, and **resource copymaster R10** for two overlapping sets.

Activity 5: Tree diagrams

Using real objects and drawing the results, let the children work on a sort to make a tree diagram. Here is an example using toy vehicles:

Activity 6: Making all the decisions

After practice the children should be able to select some things to sort, decide on the criteria for sorting, do the sort and present the outcomes in a Carroll, Venn or tree diagram. Their work can be displayed for other children to see.

Resource copymasters **R8** to **R11** may help the children record their sorts in this activity.

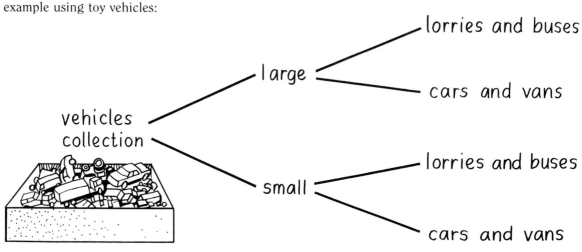

vehicles
collection

large

lorries and buses

cars and vans

small

lorries and buses

cars and vans

INTERPRETING TABLES AND LISTS

Commentary

The children may have had the opportunity to begin this work at Level 2. It is a good opportunity to revise work for some children and for you to diagnose progress made so far.

Activity 1: Looking at lists

Use the assembly of lists that you had available at Level 2. If none have been collected or saved, start a collection, which may include the following:

- Shopping lists
- Supermarket receipts
- Lists of names, like the register, or the children who are doing cooking next
- A book with an index.

Inspect and discuss a selection of lists with the children. Locate items on the lists together and then see if the children can do this for themselves. Set the children some little problems that they can solve by looking at a list.

Copymasters 67 presents an imaginary shopping list with questions attached. There is also work on the index in a book, the title of which you or the child can write in.

Activity 2: Looking at tables

Collect tables which demonstrate a variety of data in a number of ways. You may include some of the following:

- A railway timetable
- Nutritional contents in foodstuffs
- Wash instructions on washing powder or liquid.

Look at some tables with the children and work out together how to access the information in them. At Level 2 there is a suggested display of lists and tables which could be replicated here, with more challenging questions for the children.

CARD DATABASES

Commentary

To show the children the principle of ordering information to allow easy entry, access and extraction, let them handle the permanent 'hard copy' of a card index.

Activity: Using a card index

Create and use a card index which is useful, not only as a resource for this activity, but also to your class or school. You may choose, for example, to catalogue the following on a card index:

- Maths resources throughout the school
- Location of charts and posters
- Location of 'special' resources
- Infant library books
- Children's information books
- Children's pets
- Children's sports and hobbies.

Show the children how the items are arranged, how to locate what they need and how to add new information.

WORK ON A COMPUTER DATABASE

Commentary

The introduction of computers into the classrooms and the growth in availability of user-friendly software in recent years makes the use of databases an integral part of all of our experiences. It takes the slog out of the organisation of data and allows all sorts of interrogations to take place.

Activity 1: Entering information

Using the software prompts and the results of discussion with the children, you need to set up the categories of information to be collected in the database. The children can then enter their own file of data onto the database. You can relate the database to a project you are doing, or with appropriate forward planning try setting up two new databases each year. Soon the school will have a prodigious resource and files can be updated or added to year by year. Here are some starter ideas for databases:

● Ourselves: age, hair colour, eye colour, . . .
● Birds: size, habitat, colouring, wingspan, habits, diet, . . .
● Minibeasts: habitat, appearance, diet, . . .
● Weather: kinds, occurrence, effects on school-day, . . .
● Cooking/food: tried-and-tested recipes, nutrition needs of children, actual foods eaten, favourite foods, . . .

Activity 2: Accessing information
Using the software prompts let the children find things out using the database they have put on disc. For example, if you have let them create a database about their families, they should then be able to retrieve information. You need to review what is in the database and then set questions. Here are some examples:

● How many children in the class have a grandad called William?
● How many children have two sisters?
● How many children are the 'only' child in a family?
● How many children live in a house with two bedrooms?

You will need to take care that the problems you set can be solved using the database. Some problems will need two or even three 'sorts' to list the required data.

Area of study **55**	P of S **5b**	**BAR CHARTS**

C65, 66

Commentary
Bar charts differ from block graphs in that the blocks are replaced by continuous bars. The lengths of the respective bars are the means by which the charts are interpreted.

Activity 1: What does a bar chart tell us?
Give the children a ready-made bar chart, for they need to be able to interpret one before they can construct one. You could use a collection of play-dough animals or cakes to set beside a bar chart made about them. Then the children will be able to see the basis for the table. Let a number of children each choose their favourite from the array of animals or cakes. The bar chart may then look like this:

Favourite cakes in the class shop

How many times chosen

Class cakes

70

Activity 2: Constructing a bar chart

Now use another collection, similar to the one used in Activity 1, and let the children set out a bar chart. For example, you may use a selection of 'stock' from a class play shop. The resulting bar chart may look something like this:

Activity 3: Bar charts from beginning to end

Help the children decide on a category of data they may collect to put on a bar chart. Here are some starter suggestions:

- Favourite dinners
- Favourite colours
- What I want to be when I am grown up
- Hours of TV viewed in a week.

The children could work in twos, collect and collate the information (asking only a part of the class to keep the categories manageable), and compile a bar chart. These could be displayed or put into a class book.

There are axes drawn on squared paper ready for a bar chart on **copymaster 65**, and some sample problem cards on **copymaster 66**; these should be photocopied on to card, cut out and covered with adhesive film.

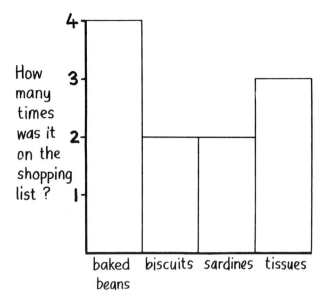

How many times was it on the shopping list?

baked beans · biscuits · sardines · tissues

Play shop stock

| Area of study 56 | P of S 5b | **SYMBOLIC PICTOGRAMS** | C68, 69 |

Commentary

The children will already be good at interpreting symbols in all areas of their lives, including in mathematics. Now is a chance to tie this work in with safety symbols, danger symbols and symbols they use in mathematics.

Activity 1: Interpreting symbols

Give the children a variety of symbols to interpret. Arrange a display of symbols which they can inspect and interpret.

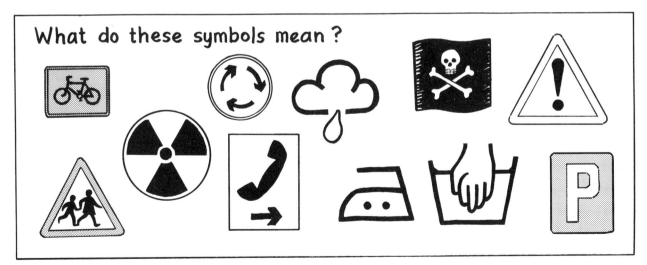

What do these symbols mean?

Activity 2: Interpreting pictograms

Show the children some ready-made pictograms with keys and help them to interpret the information.

Copymasters 68 and **69** are sample pictograms with keys. These are only examples and do not replace those you can compile using information of immediate importance to the children with whom you are working.

Activity 3: Creating symbols

Supply the children with some data which they can enter on a pictogram. For this activity they need to have the opportunity to create the symbol they will use. Here are some sample data worked through.

71

Data: **7** children clean their teeth once a day
15 children clean their teeth twice a day
4 children clean their teeth more than twice

Symbol : 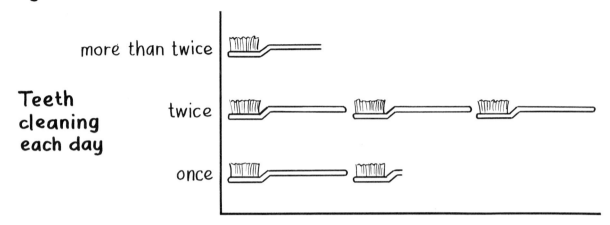 = **5 children**

Pictogram:

Teeth cleaning each day

more than twice

twice

once

Activity 4: Creating pictograms

Let the children decide on the kind of data they can collect which will be suitable for a pictogram. Help them to compile a collecting sheet for the information.

The children could work in pairs for this task. When they have the information they can collate it, devise a symbol, or symbols for it and draw up the pictogram. Here is a compilation of the steps involved.

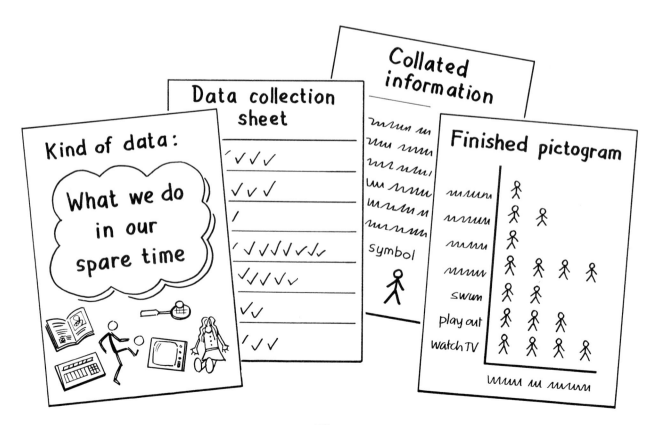

72

Shape, Space and Measures

Shape, space and measures is one of the two major building blocks of mathematics, the other being *number*. It is possible to express an awareness of two- and three-dimensional relationships without a sophisticated number system. Prehistoric cave paintings illustrate this point very well, as do early examples of sculpture and carving. Early measurements were done with locally produced units which often used the human body as a 'rule of thumb'. But trade between communities, combined with a growing desire to understand more about natural phenomena, led to the introduction of standard units of measurement. It is important, in order for children to grasp the meaning of standard units, for them to emulate their ancestors and gain experience in creating and using their own units of measurement.

In studying shape and space, children and adults are opening up their appreciation of a range of relationships to do with the natural and designed worlds. Starting from an appreciation of ourselves as having a three-dimensional existence we can move outwards to relationships with others, expressed perhaps in dance or sport. We can locate ourselves, our home, our town through maps and mapping to our country and our location on the planet Earth. Earth in space, galaxies and the universe all become part of our understanding of spatial relationships. We can take our appreciation of relationships and patterns within ourselves right down to the molecules and atoms of which all matter is made.

Shape and space, then, is not a matter of being able to identify a limited range of named shapes such as triangles and squares – although the acquisition of this sort of knowledge is important in that it allows an analysis of complex patterns in terms of constituent shapes. Shape and space work should be seen as offering experience from which children can produce increasingly more sophisticated constructions and analyses of two- and three-dimensional structures.

Resourcing shape, space and measures

In addition to the equipment listed in the resource bank at the front of the book, the following will be useful in work on shape and space:

● Paper, with squares of different sizes, 'dotty' papers (see **resource copymasters R4–R7**)
● Constructional materials ranging from paper and

plastic straws through to some sets of commercially produced constructional equipment
● Accurate mathematical shapes like Logiblocks® or Poleidoblocs® and shape templates of different shapes and in different colours, including quadrilaterals (some of which are rectangles and squares), circles and ellipses, triangles (some of which are right-angled), pentagons and hexagons
● Plasticised mirrors
● A collection of natural and designed objects demonstrating a range of shapes and posters showing examples of designed and natural structures (e.g. bridges and beehives)
● Magnetic compasses, compass designs like those on maps, a weather vane and a globe
● Set-squares with different angles.

Collections of cartons and packaging should include cubes and cuboids (boxes), cylinders (drinking straws, dowel, cylindrical containers), prisms (chocolate boxes). Add to these a sphere (table tennis ball, marbles, globe), a cone (ice-cream wafer) and a pyramid (home-made or chocolate box). Work in shape and space connects with work in science, technology and art, and materials for these areas of the curriculum will also be useful in mathematics.

In addition to all these things the following will help with specific activities in this section:

● Screws, screwdrivers, screw-top jars, keys, clock-work toys
● Sand trays, a tambour, feely bags
● An Anglepoise lamp, angle iron, information books about angled decks on aircraft and angular distance
● LOGO software and 'turtle' robot
● Books about pattern
● Plastic and real coins
● Rules and tapes (both metric and imperial)
● Containers of different shapes and volumes, and measuring jugs
● Kitchen scales and bathroom scales and standard weights
● Egg timers and interval timers and the raw materials to make sand, water and candle clocks, clocks and stopwatches and play clock faces
● Some pendulum and rocker devices and timers.

Attainment target 3: Shape, Space and Measures

Level descriptions

Level 1

When working with 3-D and 2-D shapes, pupils use everyday language to describe properties and positions. They measure and order objects using direct comparison, and order events.

Level 2

Pupils use mathematical names for common 3-D and 2-D shapes and describe their properties, including numbers of sides and corners. They distinguish between straight and turning movements, understand angle as a measurement of turn, and recognise right angles in turns. They have begun to use everyday non-standard and standard units to measure length and mass.

Level 3

Pupils classify 3-D and 2-D shapes in various ways using mathematical properties such as reflective symmetry. They use non-standard units and standard metric units of length, capacity, mass and time, in a range of contexts.

Programme of study: Shape, space and measures

■ **1. Pupils should be given opportunities to:**

a gain a wide range of practical experience using a variety of materials;

b use IT devices, *eg programmable toys, turtle graphics packages*;

c use purposeful contexts for measuring.

For this first part of the Programme of study we have set down examples drawn from the body of the book which will meet these points:

a   Area of study 1

b   Area of study 15

c   Area of study 22

Shape, space and measures

Points in the Programme of study		Areas of study and 'best fit' with level descriptions		
		Level description 1	Level description 2	Level description 3
■ 2. Understanding and using patterns and properties of shape	**a** describe and discuss shapes and patterns that can be seen or visualised;	1		
	b make common 3-D and 2-D shapes and models, working with increasing care and accuracy; begin to classify shapes according to mathematical criteria;	2, 3		
	c recognise and use the geometrical features of shapes, including vertices, sides/edges and surfaces, rectangles (including squares), circles, triangles, cubes, cuboids, progressing to hexagons, pentagons, cylinders and spheres; recognise reflective symmetry in simple cases.		4, 5	6, 7, 8
■ 3 Understanding and using properties of position and movement	**a** describe positions, using common words; recognise movements in a straight line, ie translations, and rotations, and combine them in simple ways; copy, continue and make patterns;	9, 10	11	
	b choose and use simple measuring instruments, reading and interpreting numbers and scales with some accuracy.		12, 13, 14	15
■ 4 Understanding and using measures	**a** compare objects and events using appropriate language, by direct comparison, and then using common non-standard and standard units of length, mass and capacity, *eg 'three-and-a-bit metres long', 'as heavy as 10 conkers', 'about three beakers full'*; begin to use a wider range of standard units, including standard units of time, choosing units appropriate to a situation; estimate with these units;	16, 17, 18	19, 20, 21	22, 23, 24
	b understand angle as a measure of turn and recognise quarter-turns and half-turns, *eg giving instructions for rotating a programmable toy*; recognise right angles.			25

75

Programme of study: Shape, space and measures

Pupils should be taught to:

■ **2. Understanding and using patterns and properties of shape**

a describe and discuss shapes and patterns that can be seen or visualised;

Area of study 1	P of S 2a	LD 1

NOTICING AND NAMING SHAPES ▶

Commentary

The intentions here are two-fold. First, the children should be made aware of some of the shapes around them, and reminded of what they know about these shapes. As you are 'raising awareness' try not to limit the kinds of responses children make. All that they can say about a shape will help to enlarge their intellectual map of that shape.

Secondly, you are beginning an induction of the children into new perspectives and new ways of describing their world. It does have some jargon attached, and so they do need to learn the mathematical names for shapes. However, the name for a shape and its distinguishing features (which children will have the opportunity to learn at Level 2) are but a small part of what children need to know.

Work with small groups where possible, because all the children will want a 'go' and it is important that they handle the shapes in collections and on displays.

Technically speaking, a thin flat plastic shape and a shape drawing on paper are not two-dimensional, for the plastic has thickness, as does the ink and paper. Except for high precision work in, for example, micro-engineering, we accept 'flat' shapes as two-dimensional.

Activity 1: Shape awareness

Ask the children what they understand by 'shape' and discuss with them some of the shapes they know. They may have idiosyncratic ways of naming shapes and of comparing them. Collect together and discuss all the words they use, including things like 'lumpy', 'curvy', 'pointed' and even emotive words like 'scary', 'kind', 'comfortable'. Record the discussions in a concertina book or chart for the start of a display.

Activity 2: Matching 3-D shapes

From your shape and space resource box take a number of real cartons and containers. Now play games like these:

● *Match the shape* – Pick one up and the children can pick one out to match.
● *Which shape is missing?* – Take away a shape, while the children close their eyes, and they point to one like the one missing.

● *Create a feely bag* (a borrowed shoe bag works well) and place a shape or collection of shapes in the bag unseen. The children can take it in turns to try to match a shape on the table with a shape in the bag, either by feeling through the fabric of the bag or by putting their hand inside.

Include in the collection at least the following shapes, though the children may not need to name them all at this level:

> Cuboid
> Cube
> Cylinder
> Prisms with triangular and
> hexagonal bases
> Sphere
> Cone.

When not in use lay the shapes out on a display table so that the children can handle them.

There are 3 shapes in the feely bag

Can you find matching shapes on the shape table ?

Activity 3: Naming 2-D shapes

Assemble a collection of two-dimensional shapes, including the following, though the children may not be able to name them all:

> Rectangle
> Square
> Circle
> Triangle
> Hexagon
> Pentagon.

Play games similar to those in Activity 2. Mount a display where the shapes can be touched when not in use, and named, if you feel the children are ready to name them.

Activity 4: Shapes around the school

Let the children look around the school, both inside and out, and spot as many shapes as they can. They can have a go at first recording by drawing some of the shapes they see on paper. For a report-back session have a large sectioned piece of paper ready. You can then label the children's sketches and cut them out to assemble in the set of the correct shape.

Give the children a little picture quiz called 'Find the shape'. Tell them where the answers are likely to be – not too far away from the classroom! You could include, for example, a drawing of the framed picture in the corridor, the caretaker's broomstick, the door to the playground and the shape of the window.

Activity 5: Shape collections

Create a shape collecting point, and invite children to bring in packaging suitable for junk modelling. When you have a mountain of shapes, let the children sort them out. Choose the best examples for the resource box and put the others aside for some of the activities to come.

Start a collection of natural shapes which the children can handle. Include, for example, a blown egg, a starfish, angular pieces of rock, a hollow log, a palmate leaf, a snail shell. In fact you can include any natural shape which will get the children talking and collecting.

Arrange a complementary display of manufactured shapes. These could include a sole for a shoe, a piece of raw spaghetti, plastic tubing, a cardboard box, a plastic bottle, a kite, coins, a belt and a headscarf.

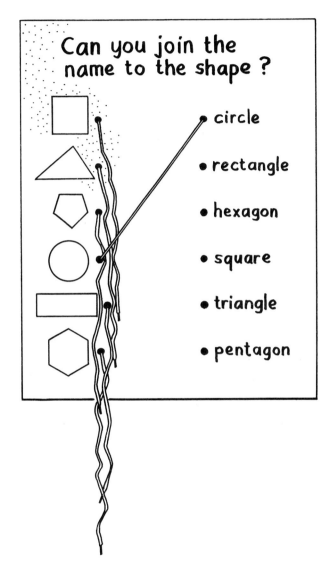

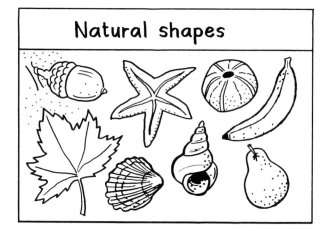

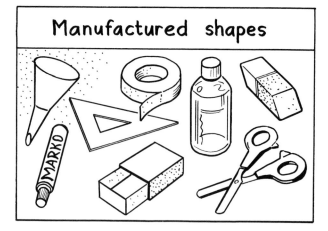

Programme of study: Shape, space and measures

Pupils should be taught to:

■ **2. Understanding and using patterns and properties of shape**

b make common 3-D and 2-D shapes and models, working with increasing care and accuracy; begin to classify shapes according to mathematical criteria;

Area of study 2	P of S 2b	LD 1

BUILDING 3-D SHAPES

Commentary

Before children learn about maths they almost all have had experience of building *with* shapes, which is the place to begin this part of their work. However, you need to be aware that because of traditional expectations and stereotyping, some girls may have not had much opportunity for constructional play. Boys are still the ones who are commonly and routinely given construction opportunities.

It is worth giving children support in junk model-making, partly because they can talk and learn while they work and also because cartons turned inside out and re-stuck (by an adult) take paint reasonably well and look much more attractive.

W(o)W! Wonderful models!
* Which have cuboids in them?
* Which was hardest to build?

78

Activity 1: Building *with* shapes

Provide the children with a wide range of three-dimensional shapes with which to build. You can do much with junk modelling materials, and the pleasure in these is that they form an eye-catching display, a talking point for you and the children (for example: 'What shape is the wheel on Ernie's tractor?') and they can be taken home.

Duplo®, Lego®, Multilink®, wooden bricks, and other commercially available construction toys can be used to good effect in temporary model-making. There are also sets of building shapes on the market which children love to play with and have the features of 'mathematical' shapes. Poliedoblocs® is one such commercially available set.

Activity 2: Building cuboids and cubes

Lego® is the obvious resource to use. Many of the pieces are cuboid (if you ignore the dimples), and solid and hollow cuboids can be made using them.

Lego® or wooden blocks can give children the opportunity to construct cubes. When they have played, give them challenges like: 'Can you build a smaller one? How many pieces do you think are in the shape you have built?'.

Activity 3: Building cylinders

Curl paper and ribbon and let the children make paper sculptures.

Let the children try making a cylinder shape from heavy rope. Display this and then show them how to decorate an empty tin (with a safe top edge) with coloured wools and strings. Let the children make play paper telescopes and clay coil pots.

Activity 4: Building prisms

These shapes are quite hard to build. Try using strips of card, folded to match a size strip. Fold into shape and stick. They will then make good collages or mobiles, or could be stuck together to make a tunnel or roof.

Activity 5: Building spheres

Play dough, Plasticine® and clay are possible media here. You can also try cooking things like raspberry buns and ginger nuts where the dough has to be rolled into balls before being placed on the baking sheet.

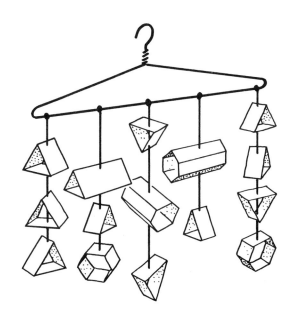

79

Activity 6: Skeleton shapes

Using Artstraws® or paper drinking straws, help the children to make a few skeleton shapes, including a cube, a cuboid and a pyramid. The children may find this difficult without adult help.

There are construction sets available which may be easier for the children to handle; they include plastic straws and connectors.

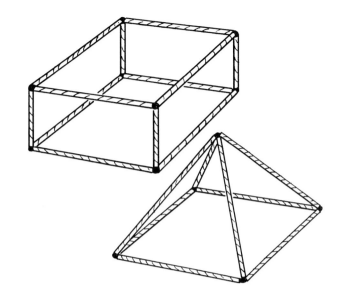

Activity 7: Irregular shapes

When the opportunity arises point out to the children that not all shapes are regular, but that they need to have certain features to belong to a shape family. This is laying the foundations for work at Level 2.

Area of study	P of S	LD		
3	2b	1	**DRAWING 2-D SHAPES**	C 70

Commentary

Children's hand control skills may be limited when they are ready for this work. They should, however, be able to do a rough but recognisable sketch of shapes they see. This is quite adequate at this stage.

There is a challenge for you to find as many ways of recording shape, other than drawing, as you can.

Activity 1: 'Magic finger' drawing

Ask the children to draw shapes as you draw them, with a 'magic finger' in the air. Draw with fingers in other media, like sand and chalk dust.

Activity 2: Draw what you see

Show the children a collection of card or plastic shapes and let them draw what they see. They can create pictures composed entirely of the shapes on the table.

Copymaster 70 (Shape pictures) is a drawing sheet using shape.

Activity 3: Drawing round

Give the children the same kinds of shapes as in Activity 2 above and let them draw round them to produce pictures. Set the children open-ended

challenges like: 'Draw a monkey, or a petrol station, or a playground.' Also set some that are structured; for example, 'Draw a supermarket shelf of food using rectangles and squares, or a nest of chicks using circles and ovals.'

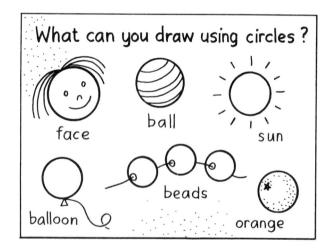

What can you draw using circles?

face   ball   sun

balloon   beads   orange

What shapes have we drawn in the sand trays?

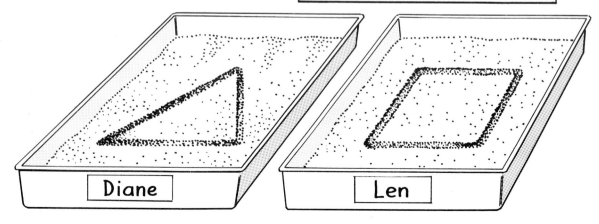

Diane   Len

80

Activity 4: Painting and printing

Paint shapes with fingers and brushes, using powder paint, water colours, fluorescent paint. Rub a candle really hard over a shape under a piece of paper – colour wash over it and the shape will appear. Paint sequences of shapes to make border designs and repeat patterns. Try painting a single shape in different positions and using different colours.

Print with sponges, boxes, ends of cylinders, coins (stuck on boxes), wooden sticks, ends of pencils and pen tops. Produce repeat patterns, patterns of size, borders and random patterns. Create galaxies and bubble baths, building sites and boxes of toys, aviaries and shelves of books. The children's art links shape and space and pattern to the real world.

Activity 5: Sticky shapes

Use ready-cut sticky shapes to produce pictures, patterns and mosaics. The latter is a direct experience of tessellation which the children will tackle at Level 5.

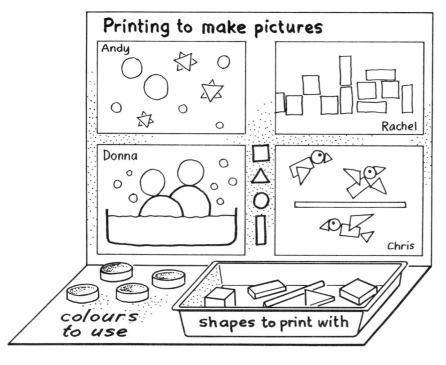

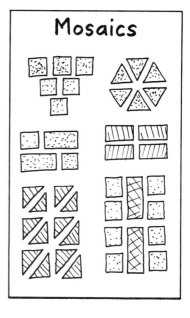

Programme of study: Shape, space and measures

Pupils should be taught to:

■ **2. Understanding and using patterns and properties of shape**

c recognise and use the geometrical features of shapes, including vertices, sides/edges and surfaces, rectangles (including squares), circles, triangles, cubes, cuboids, progressing to hexagons, pentagons, cylinders and spheres; recognise reflective symmetry in simple cases.

2-D SHAPES

C71
–73

Commentary

With work at Level 1 covered thoroughly, the children should sail through these activities. They offer an opportunity for you to consolidate work at Level 1 and identify any children who have not yet truly grasped some of the basic principles.

Activity 1: The language of shape

Both you and the children will probably use words other than shape names in your mathematical discussions. Now is the opportunity to ensure that the children fully understand a wide range of words used in talking about shapes.

Introduce all of these to the children:

- corner (and, if they arise, point, vertex)
- side (2-D) and edge (3-D)
- face
- three-dimensional ('back', 'front' and 'thickness')
- two-dimensional (no 'thickness').

Place a number of boxes and cartons or plastic or card shapes on the table, and ask a child to point to, for example, one with four corners, one with more than four faces, a shape with six sides and so on. The children will enjoy setting this kind of problem for one another.

Activity 2: Shapes in class

Now that the children have some maths language for shapes and their features, you can encourage them to look for shapes around the room. Ask them to work in pairs to spot as many of one shape as they can in a couple of minutes. Assemble their results by drawing sketches of what they spotted, or combining these with pictures cut from magazines.

Activity 3: Work with squares and rectangles

Use a collection of flat plastic shapes, which should include a number of squares and rectangles and irregular quadrilaterals and parallelograms. From these the children, working in a small group, can make selections. Choose a square from the collection, and without saying what it is called, ask each child to find another like it. If the children can name it, ask them to tell you about it. A child may say, 'It has four corners.' You can then pick up an irregular quadrilateral and ask, 'Is this a square?' Gradually the children will be able to say what the key attributes are that identify a square (namely four sides of equal length and four corners the same).

Now play the same game, choosing a rectangle from the collection, and eventually helping the children to understand that a rectangle has two pairs of sides with equal lengths and four corners the same.

Start a shape identifier book.

Activity 4: Work with triangles

Use a collection of triangles cut from card and plastic. Make sure there is a range including equilateral (sides of equal length), right-angled and some with very acute angles. Add a few shapes that are not triangles to the collection. Using the same game as in Activity 1 help the children to establish what the crucial attributes of a triangle are (namely that it has three sides!). You do not need to ask the children to distinguish between kinds of triangles at this stage.

Activity 5: Work with circles

Use a collection of circles, ovals and ellipses for this game. Just ensure that the children can pick out a circle from a collection. They need only be able to distinguish it at this stage, and not name its attributes.

82

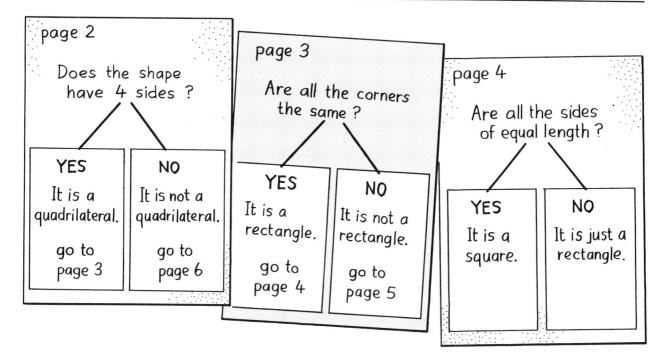

page 2

Does the shape have 4 sides ?

YES	NO
It is a quadrilateral.	It is not a quadrilateral.
go to page 3	go to page 6

page 3

Are all the corners the same ?

YES	NO
It is a rectangle.	It is not a rectangle.
go to page 4	go to page 5

page 4

Are all the sides of equal length ?

YES	NO
It is a square.	It is just a rectangle.

Activity 6: Work with hexagons and pentagons

Create a collection of shapes with many sides and of varying sizes. Include hexagons and pentagons. If the children can pick these shapes out of the collection, see if they can identify the attribute they are using to choose the appropriate shape. If they cannot choose the appropriate shape, take one yourself, name it, and get the children to find one that matches. Talk together about how to find this shape among others.

Copymasters 71–73 let the children match attributes to shapes. **Copymasters 72** and **73** should be photocopied on to card, and the small cards on copymaster 73 cut out; a child can then match these to the attributes printed on the board of copymaster 72.

3-D SHAPES

Commentary

The children may be familiar with some of the names of these shapes, though they may have forgotten the word 'cuboid' as it is not used very often in everyday speech.

Check that the children are confident about using shape vocabulary, including 'face', 'side', 'edge' and 'corner'.

There are, in fact, only five *regular* three-dimensional shapes. We do not intend that you should teach the children these shapes but it is important to see the direction of some aspects of three-dimensional work. The regular solids are:

● *Cube.* Six faces, each face being a square. Three faces meet at each corner or vertex.
● *Tetrahedron.* Four faces, each face being an equilateral triangle. Three faces meet at each vertex.
● *Octahedron.* Eight faces, each face being an equilateral triangle. Four faces meet at each vertex. (A regular octahedron can be made by sticking two similar square-based pyramids together, whose edges are all equal.)
● *Icosahedron.* Twenty faces, each face being an equilateral triangle. Five faces meet at each vertex.
● *Dodecahedron.* Twelve faces, each face being a pentagon. Three faces meet at each vertex.

A sphere shares with the regular solids the characteristic that its shape does not change, you just get larger or smaller versions of spheres. But spheres do not have plane faces. When you take a section across a sphere the plane cut is always a circle.

Activity 1: Work with cubes and cuboids

From the resource box assemble a collection of cartons, boxes and mathematical shapes which are shaped like a cube or cuboid. The children may be able to sort out the cubes and say what distinguishes them from the other shapes.

Make a list of all the things the children know that come in cube shapes. Add these to a class chart or display.

Now do the same activity with cuboids. Finally set a cube beside a cuboid and look for differences.

Copymaster 74 presents some work on cubes and cuboids.

Activity 2: Work with cylinders

From the resource box assemble a collection of cylinders. To the ubiquitous paper roll centres and chocolate bean containers, do not forget to add a piece of dowel and a broomstick! Ask the children to look at what distinguishes a cylinder from other shapes. See if they can predict what a cylinder will look like if it is laid out flat. Cut and open out a paper cylinder to show them. Arrange a display to include some cylinders that children may have failed to notice.

Copymaster 75 presents some work with cylinders.

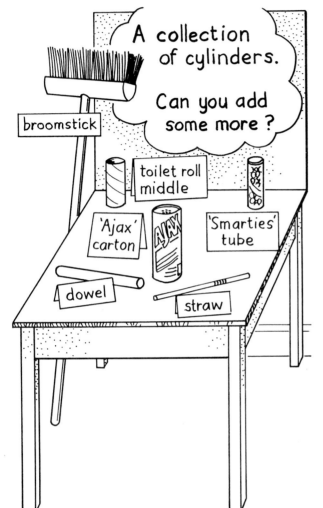

Activity 3: Work with spheres

Not many things are packaged in spherical containers. If they fill a box with cuboids, and then with spheres the children may be able to work out why that is. Balls of Plasticine®, marbles, a football, a tennis ball and a globe will be a big enough collection for children to examine. You do not need to discuss the properties of spheres further at this stage.

Add the spheres to the classroom display for a while.

Copymasters C76–78 provide a game for two to four players based on recognition of two-dimensional representations of three-dimensional shapes. Photocopy all three masters on to card. Cut up the shape cards on copymaster C78 and the four game boards on copymasters C76 and C77. Place the shape cards face down, spread over the table (as in 'Memory match' games). Each player in turn picks up one card; if it is one they need for the model on their game board, they keep it; otherwise, they replace the card on the table. The winner is the first player to collect all the shapes needed for their model.

Area of study 6	P of S 2c	LD 3	**SORTING 2-D SHAPES**	C79, R4–7

Commentary

In many respects this work maps closely on to the work in Level 2. It is very much a consolidation of those earlier activities and provides you with an opportunity to remediate and/or extend the appreciation of two-dimensional shapes.

Activity 1: Sorting out

Using a selection of card and plastic two-dimensional shapes, sort them into sets. Ask the children to guess how they have been sorted. Let the children take it in turns to do the sort.

Arrange a display of the shapes when not in use so that the children can freely examine and sort them.

Activity 2: Attributes shapes

Buy or borrow a set of shapes, or better still, several sets of shapes that are mathematically accurate. Do 'sorts' with these. It will depend on what the set contains what 'sorts' are possible. Make sure that the children can recognise and identify right angles (Level 2), sides of equal length and numbers of corners or vertices.

Activity 3: Attributes quiz

Set the children a quiz which involves identifying shapes according to their attributes. For example, you could ask: 'Name two shapes which have four corners.' 'What is a shape with six sides called?'

There is a two-dimensional shapes quiz on **copymaster 79**.

Activity 4: LOGO

Set up the computer with LOGO software, and invite the children to produce shapes that are mathematically correct. The results can be printed out alongside the program invented, and this can be tried out by other children. Depending on their experience with computers and with LOGO (see Level 2), the children may need some help from you to make a start. This activity also helps to refine logical thinking.

Activity 5: Shape and pattern investigation

Make a collection of books about ancient civilisations, other cultures and pattern in art, and invite the children to choose a pattern and investigate its origins, or a civilisation or culture and investigate the patterns used. If the children are not ready for research in this way, choose, for example, 'The ancient Egyptians', 'Patterns from the East', or 'North American Indians' and find out some of the main pattern forms in use. With the stimulus of books, pictures, fabrics and

maybe even objects with patterns on them, the children will be able to explore and replicate the shapes used in pattern-making. The outcome would make a stunning display.

You may find the children enjoy producing patterns on squared paper (**resource copymasters R4** and **R5**) or on 'dotty' paper (**resource copymasters R6** and **R7**).

Area of study 7	P of S 2c	LD 3

SORTING 3-D SHAPES

Commentary

Again we are looking at the consolidation of earlier work. The children should now be coming to a skilled recognition of similarities and differences between three-dimensional shapes. They should be recognising and naming shapes and be able to pick out shapes in the environment.

Activity 1: Sorting out

Use a collection of cartons, boxes and containers to make shape sets. Let the children identify the basis for the sort, and then do 'sorts' for themselves.

Activity 2: Attributes blocks

Using a set of shapes that are mathematically accurate, like Logiblocks® (which offer not only shape, but size, colour and thickness) or Poleidoblocs® (which include cones and pyramids), let the children do the sorting using one or more criteria (see Area of study 46). They can record some of the outcomes of the sorts using Venn or Carroll diagrams, for example.

Resource copymasters R8–10 (Venn diagrams) and **R11** (Carroll diagram) will help children with their recording of sorts.

Activity 3: Attributes quiz

Give the children a quiz involving the attributes of three-dimensional shapes. You could ask, for example: 'Which shape has two triangular faces?' and 'Which shapes have eight corners?'

Copymaster 80 is a three-dimensional shapes quiz.

Activity 4: Shape in buildings

Look at the school buildings and those in neighbouring streets and determine the shapes in common use. Discuss with the children why these shapes are used. Ask the children to draw buildings using shapes different from those they have seen, and to comment on the advantages and disadvantages of the new shapes.

Activity 5: The shape of our school

Make a model of the school. It need not be accurately to scale for the children may find accurate measurement difficult at this stage, but the shape must reflect the actual look of the school. Display the model with a discussion of the process of modelling and the kinds of shapes that had to be considered and incorporated.

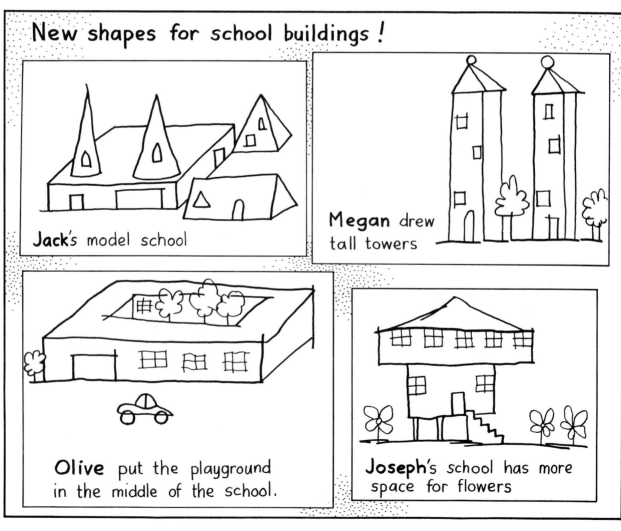

New shapes for school buildings !

Jack's model school

Megan drew tall towers

Olive put the playground in the middle of the school.

Joseph's school has more space for flowers

Activity 6: The built environment

Look at buildings around the school, particularly those with a variety of shapes in them. You may, for example, be near the village church or the market cross, the Corn Exchange, mill or Town Hall. The children may want to investigate shapes in popular use a long time ago.

Activity 7: Model-making

When setting children model-making tasks, you can use shape names and attributes, and expect quite sophisticated outcomes. You can tie this work in with their technology activities. Here are some examples of the kinds of tasks to set:

- Archways and tunnels
- Towers

- Structures that lean
- Structures that have a small base and large top.

In all cases the children can display and discuss their efforts.

Activity 8: Shape in everyday expressions

With the children's help, collect together sayings and expressions which use shape and space in the wording. Discuss what we mean when we use these. Examples include:

- 'It is as broad as it is long'
- 'Get to the point'
- 'Rounding off'
- 'Keep to the straight and narrow'
- 'There is no side to her'
- 'Being on edge'.

Area of study	P of S	LD
8	2c	3

SYMMETRY

C81 –84

Commentary

The two forms of symmetry that children will identify given the opportunity are line or reflective symmetry and rotational symmetry. Of these it is expected that reflective symmetry will be commonly recognised by children at this Level.

Reflective symmetry means that a line drawn through a shape will give two halves of the shape which are mirror images of each other. An example would be a line through the centre of the unequal side of an isoceles triangle and the opposite angle. An equilateral triangle has three lines of symmetry. A circle has an infinite number.

Rotational symmetry means that a shape can be rotated and at certain positions will look like the shape at its starting point. Examples are the letter S and a child's windmill.

Activity 1: Ink-blots and butterflies

Cut paper to various shapes and sizes. Make sure the paper is partially absorbent, that is, neither too glossy nor too absorbent, or it will make this task difficult for the children to do without making a mess. Fold each piece along the centre line. Let the children put blobs of paint or water-based ink on the paper, and then fold it along the crease and rub gently to spread the paint or ink a little. When they open up the paper the resulting picture has two matching halves (one axis of symmetry). This work can be used for book covers, mobiles and display.

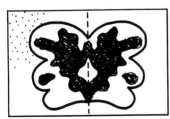 

Patterns with one axis of symmetry

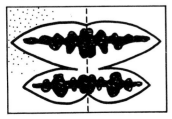 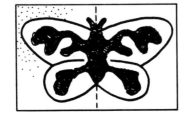

Activity 2: Cutting folded paper

Cut paper to various shapes and sizes. Fold the paper along a centre line. Ask the children to cut out a shape, through both thicknesses, starting by cutting across the fold. When the paper is opened out the children will see that the fold marks the axis of symmetry of the picture.

Activity 3: 2-D shapes with one axis of symmetry

Supply the children with a box of two-dimensional shapes and some plane 'plastic' mirrors. Let them explore with shapes they can put the mirror on, and re-create the shape perfectly.

Copymaster 81 (2-D shapes and symmetry) offers children a range of shapes and they can decide which are symmetrical (some have more than one axis of symmetry).

Activity 4: Folding shapes

Give the children some scraps of paper which are irregular shapes, and some regular shaped pieces. Ask them to try folding the pieces of paper, to see which offer symmetrical halves and which do not.

Activity 5: Symmetry, pairs and left and right

Show the children that one axis of symmetry offers two halves which match, and that this match marks a left and a right as in feet, shoes, hands, mittens and eyes! Practise left and right and give the children the chance to match their own lefts and rights on a display.

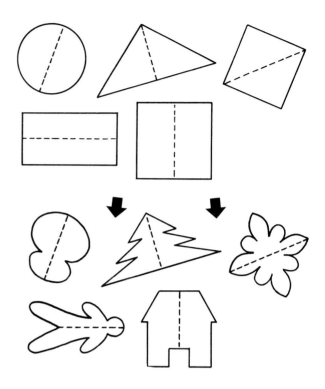

On the classroom door, on the side where the door opens away (so that the children do not get hit on the nose!) stick down two giant footprints on the floor. Mark these left and right. On the door attach two giant hands and mark them left and right. Cover them with clear film for they will get a lot of use. The children can stand on the giant footprints and match their hands to the handprints.

Activity 6: 2-D shapes with more than one axis of symmetry

Check out all the shapes in your classroom collection with the children to see which have more than one axis of symmetry. Create a symmetry classbook that offers puzzles and shape facts to the children.

Activity 7: Symmetry in numerals

Let the children draw and colour the numerals 1 to 10, or their age numeral, or the number of their house, and then work out and draw in the axes of symmetry in these, if any.

Copymaster 82 (House number symmetry) is a sheet on which to record their own or their friend's house number, and then look at what they can do to it with a plane mirror.

Activity 8: Symmetry in letters

Let the children draw and embellish their own name in capital letters. They can then see which letters have axes of symmetry and where the axes lie.

Copymaster 83 (Letter symmetry) gives the children the chance to play with axes of symmetry in letters of their own name using a plane mirror.

Activity 9: 3-D shapes and planes of symmetry

Try cutting a matchbox, a cuboid of cheese, an apple or orange and a (firm!) marshmallow across some of their planes of symmetry and showing them to the children. If you can get hold of matching food boxes, you can lay them together, pretend they are one box, and then show a plane of symmetry where they part.

Planes of symmetry are quite difficult to demonstrate in a drawing. With your help, and using straws or card strips, the children could make skeleton models of, for example, a cuboid, a cube, a prism and a pyramid. Using pieces of thin paper, you can demonstrate where the planes of symmetry lie.

Another possibility is for you yourself to cut Plasticine® shapes through the planes of symmetry.

Copymaster 84 (Planes of symmetry) gives children the chance to enter how many planes of symmetry are found in some shapes.

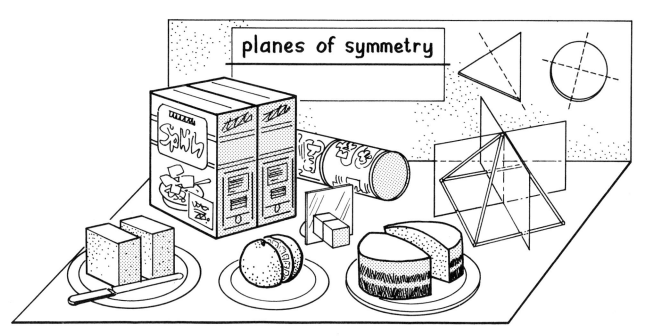

Programme of study: Shape, space and measures

Pupils should be taught to:

■ **3. Understanding and using patterns and properties of shape**

a describe positions, using common words; recognise movements in a straight line, ie translations, and rotations, and combine them in simple ways; copy, continue and make patterns;

Area of study	P of S	LD
9	3a	1

DESCRIBING POSITION

C 85

Commentary

Explore the language we use to describe position. The first steps in such an exploration are to start with a few variables. Here we are concerned with a discussion of fixed positions and not the movement between one position and another.

Activity 1: Position words

The children will already know many position words. Play guessing games like 'Where is the book?' 'Where is the doll?' 'Where is the headteacher?' Encourage the children to use words like:

up/down
under/over
above/below
beside
in front of/behind
on top of/underneath.

Ask two children to stand facing the others. Move the children's hands or legs into position and tell the class: 'Tracy's leg is beside Hannah's. Hannah's hand is above Tracy's', and so on. Then give Hannah and Tracy directions, so that they can move into position to match the instructions.

Ask the group of children to work in pairs, and give one of each pair a red sticker. The others should have a blue sticker. Now give directions to the whole group. For example, you may say, 'Blues stand in front of reds. Reds crouch down while blues stand up.'

Put all this position vocabulary into a classbook and add it to the book corner.

Activity 2: Position quiz

Make a set of simple picture clues that match to things around the room. Ask the children, a pair at a time, to find where the clues go.

To help recognition, **copymaster 85** (Position words) is a set of pictures with position words attached which the children can ring.

Area of study	P of S	LD	
10	3a	1	**MOVING POSITION**

Commentary

Here we start to combine position vocabulary with movement. In moving it is important to stress the idea of *rotation*. This is in order to give the children a good platform for when they encounter the idea of an angle.

Activity 1: Position in PE and dance

During PE lessons, plan work specifically to cover position words. Starter games include 'Statues' and 'Machines'. Once the children have had a few sessions at exploring these, you can begin to set quite detailed limits to the position they adopt when you stop their movement by giving a clap. For example, you could say: 'I should like you to move around as fast as you can, and when I clap I want you to be a statue looking up and pushing down' or 'When I clap, the machine must do two lifting-up movements and then stop.'

Help the children to invent a simple dance routine based on a few position words, set it to music and work it into an assembly called perhaps 'Going shopping' or 'Exploring the jungle.'

Activity 2: Position in play

In the play activities set for the children, you can ensure that there is a full range of position words, and directions to change position.

Activity 3: Program a robot

Let the children have a go at giving instructions to a programmable robot (there are a number available through educational suppliers). See if the children can get the robot to follow a route describing a shape, or master a simple obstacle course.

Area of study	P of S	LD	
11	3a	2	**MOVEMENT**

Commentary

Now is the time to set the groundwork for work on symmetry at Level 3 and beyond.

Work on movement can tie in with ideas related to repeat patterns in algebra.

Underlying our power to conserve length, capacity and weight is an understanding of position and orientation, which can be developed through moving ourselves and objects around us.

Activity 1: Kinds of movement in PE

During a series of PE lessons, explain to the children the kinds of movement there are. These can be named:

● *Straight movement* (translation). Marching might be seen as a straight movement.

● *Turning movement* (rotation). Ballet-type dance and graceful flowing movements involve turning of the limbs and whole body.

Include in the activities a series of movements, some involving stiff limbs and rigid taut bodies, and some graceful and flowing involving swirling and turning arms, legs, hands, feet and bodies.

Activity 2: Kinds of movement in art

The distinctions made in kinds of movement done in

PE in Activity 1 can be illustrated through art. Here are some examples:

● *Translation.* Straight strokes with a brush, using large sheets of paper. This makes excellent wrapping, book covers, backdrops for collage or abstract work.

● *Rotation.* Curling and turning, spirals in paint and print, taking your brush in any path across the paper, turning and printing, angles in prints.

Activity 3: Moving a programmable toy

Let the children program a toy to complete straight and turning movements.

Straight movements made these patterns

Curling and turning movements made these patterns

Programme of study: Shape, space and measures

Pupils should be taught to:

■ **3. Understanding and using patterns and properties of shape**

b understand angle as a measure of turn and recognise quarter-turns and half-turns, *eg giving instructions for rotating a programmable toy;* recognise right angles.

Area of study	P of S	LD
12	3b	2

RIGHT ANGLES

C 86 –87

Commentary

It can be quite difficult to draw a shape without using a right angle. Right angles are extremely common in the built environment. 'Square' corners occur everywhere, and this makes it the best choice for starting work with the children on the notion of angle.

Activity 1: Introducing right angles

Folding a piece of paper in half and then in half again will produce a right angle. Do this with the children and tell them about the angle's special name. Ask them to search around the classroom to see where there are right angles. Compile a list of the right angles that they can find. Talk about the characteristics of a right angle after this activity.

Copymaster 86 gives practice in recording right angles.

Activity 2: Right angle search

Using two- and three-dimensional shapes from the shape resource box, let the children examine them to find right angles. They should now be able to say that squares, rectangles, cubes and cuboids all have right-angled corners, and some triangles and prisms do too.

Arrange a sorting display where the children can add to sets of shapes which have and lack right angles.

Copymaster 87 gives practice in identifying shapes with right angles.

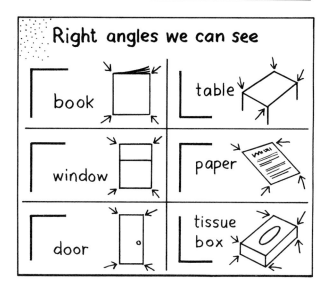

Right angles we can see

book — table — window — paper — door — tissue box

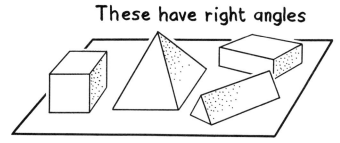

These have right angles

These do not

  ANGLE, INCLUDING RIGHT ANGLES

Area of study 13 | P of S 3b | LD 2 | C88

Commentary

It is important to see different angles as being the result of a movement – a rotation. Rather than visualising an angle as some sort of measure between two lines joined at one end it is useful to imagine that one line is moving, rather like a hand on a clock. Indeed, the movements of the hands of a clock are useful in considering the idea of angle with children. Seeing angles as connected with rotation will help with the idea of a complete (360°) turn and, at a later stage, the possibility of greater than one turn.

Activity 1: Concept of angle

In a PE lesson ask the children to move about, changing direction abruptly at the sound of a clap or tambour. When they have done this a few times point out to them that the abrupt change of direction is tracing an 'angle' on the floor. Next ask them to make angular shapes with their bodies. They can do this by themselves and then in pairs.

Activity 2: Angles around us

Ask the children to look for angles in the environment. If they have already looked for right angles this will be an extra challenge, for they can search out angles other than right angles.

Copymaster 88 (Angles around school) gives the children an opportunity to list kinds of angles they find.

Activity 3: Angle in design

Create a display to include an Anglepoise® lamp, angle iron, information about the angled deck on aircraft, and a book on astronomy explaining the use of angular distance. Add to this models of three-dimensional shapes the children have made.

Activity 4: Following angle instructions

Now that the children have learned about themselves and angle, and have experimented at making angles with their bodies in Activity 1, they should be ready to follow instructions about angle. In a series of PE floor-work lessons, try getting them to turn through right angles and acute angles to create a short movement sequence. This can be shown in an assembly, or they can translate the movements into design, using chalks, paints or collage.

Activity 5: Angles and LOGO

Let the children use a LOGO software package on the school computer to move the 'turtle' through different amounts of a rotation (size of angle) and create patterns and shapes. (See also Shape, space and measures, Area of study 15.)

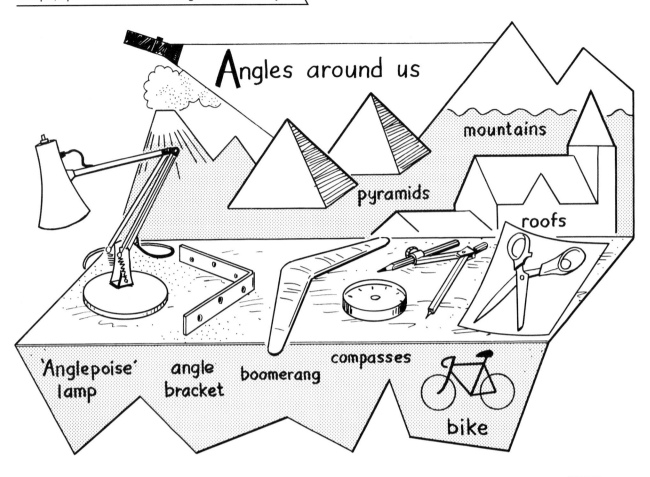

Angles around us

mountains
pyramids
roofs
'Anglepoise' lamp
angle bracket
boomerang
compasses
bike

| Area of study 14 | P of S 3b | LD 2 | **FUN WITH SHAPE AND ANGLE** | C89 |

Commentary

If you are to keep children free of the prejudice that mathematics is sums, or at best squares and circles, and keep the joy in their learning, then enabling them to have fun with shape and angle is a chance to be really creative. The following widely diverse activities will all contribute to children's confidence with shape and pattern.

Activity 1: Silly walks

(With apologies to Monty Python!) Invite the children to invent as many ways as they can of getting about. You can talk about straight and turning movements, but the important thing is that the children have a chance to experiment and recognise the possibilities in moving themselves. This understanding will feed their understanding of shape and space in mathematics.

Activity 2: Play acting moving shapes

Create a series of shape characters and invent a one-act play. The events do not need to be fantastical: 'A meal out for Ann Square' or 'The Cuboids visit the library' would provide many opportunities for shape talk and meetings.

Copymaster 89 (Shape characters and play titles) presents the children with a selection of possible characters and titles from which they may choose, and to which they may add to invent a play. These could be acted out with children dressed as the characters. Make a video of it if you can.

Activity 3: Cartoons

Let the children invent some cartoon characters and tell of their adventures. They can say the story aloud while holding up a series of pictures, or create a picture that tells a story. Examples could include a story from the planet 'Angle' or 'The 2-D cat'.

...Flat Cat crept under the door...

94

LOGO

RT (angle)	– turn right the angle given
LT (angle)	– turn left the angle given
CS	– clear screen
PU	– lift the 'pen' to stop drawing
PD	– pen down to draw
PE	– use the pen as an eraser

Commentary

LOGO is a computer language which is available in all primary schools. Unlike other programming languages it has been developed with young children in mind. The language that children need to learn in order to start to work in a LOGO environment is simple and short. As the children progress they can expand their knowledge of the available commands.

LOGO is a language which is geared to children controlling a symbol and causing it to move around the computer screen. As it does so it can leave a line of its path. This means that the children can construct all sorts of diagrams and pictures. The symbol they have to move around is a 'turtle'. There is now a range of robots available which respond to children's LOGO commands.

One particular quality of LOGO is that it is structured in such a way that children can teach the 'turtle' how to carry out sets of operations, and the 'turtle' will carry out these operations on command.

Of the instructions understood by LOGO on the computer, the following will allow the children to get started and will make it possible to produce a range of shapes:

FD (number)	– forward the number of 'steps' given
BK (number)	– backward the number of 'steps' given

Activity: Introducing LOGO

For this activity you do not need any equipment. In the hall, play a 'guide your robot home' game with the children working in small groups. One child in each group plays the part of the robot 'turtle' and the others have to give the robot directions to travel from one part of the hall to another. Put obstacles such as hoops and/or skittles in the way so that they have to cope with instructing the robot to turn right and left as well as move forward or back particular numbers of steps.

So that the children can use the 'angle' instruction within LOGO, support them in making, for example, simple bearings discs based upon circular protractors. These need not include all degrees but, in the first instance, could have some of the more useful angles such as 90°, 45°, 60°.

If you have access to a real 'robot', use it to replicate the first robot game. Free-standing robots now available will allow children to program them to move, turn and even play tunes. With a pen attachment they can also draw a path on large sheets of paper.

Programme of study: Shape, space and measures

■ **4. Understanding and using measures**

Pupils should be taught to:

a compare objects and events using appropriate language, by direct comparison, and then using common non-standard and standard units of length, mass and capacity, eg 'three-and-a-bit metres long', 'as heavy as 10 conkers', 'about three beakers full'; begin to use a wider range of standard units, including standard units of time, choosing units appropriate to a situation; estimate with these units;

TALKING ABOUT MEASURES

Commentary

This introduction to measures begins with a look at some of the everyday words we use in making comparisons of the following: dimensions, area, weight, capacity, temperature, monetary value, time and other differences. The intention is that the children should be confident with the language of measurement before they record.

Measurement is about comparison. We would say a beach ball is big when compared with a golf ball, but the golf ball is said to be big when compared with a marble. What we should be saying each time is 'bigger than'. Do not be tempted to make collections of 'light' things or 'small' things, though there can in a collection be things that are 'lighter than . . .' and you can declare something the 'lightest' on the table. Everyday comparisons are idiosyncratic, and depend on context. You depend on a common understanding of what you imply. A bag of sugar might be pronounced heavy by a five-year-old, but an adult in weight-training would not say the same. Encourage the children with their 'comparison' vocabulary, even with dimensions which they will probably not measure and quantify in the infant school, like flexibility and hardness. Work like this will reinforce measurement as being a comparison exercise, and will help their work in other subjects (for example, science AT 3, and technology).

Note that, at this stage, all is talk and 'play'. Do not make the children write anything down yet!

Activity 1: Size and coverage

Talk about size. Start with an object, for example a toy mouse or a fir cone, and discuss with the children things that are bigger than or smaller than these. You could focus the discussion by comparing the mouse with other animals they know, and the fir cone with other fruits. Continue the discussion in a series of sessions, using objects and pictures of objects, gradually exploring the vocabulary with the children. Do not forget to try a series of cloths on the play house table to see which covers it, and paper masks which may cover the face. This is just to 'set the scene' for later discussions of area.

Collect all the common words we use in talking about size. These may include:

- big/bigger/biggest, large/larger/largest
- small/smaller/smallest, little/littler/littlest
- tiny/tinier/tiniest
- long/longer/longest, short/shorter/shortest
- tall/taller/tallest, wide/wider/widest
- broad/broader/broadest
- narrow/narrower/narrowest

- thin/thinner/thinnest, fat/fatter/fattest
- high/higher/highest, low/lower/lowest.

Make a class folder or book with all these words in it. Develop the concepts further in the activities under 'Compare and order' below.

Activity 2: How heavy?

As in Activity 1, use a collection of objects to elicit everyday words about 'weight' from the children. These will include the following:

- weigh, balance, scales, pointer, dial
- light/lighter/lightest, heavy/heavier/heaviest.

Make a class folder of key words, for use in 'Compare and order'.

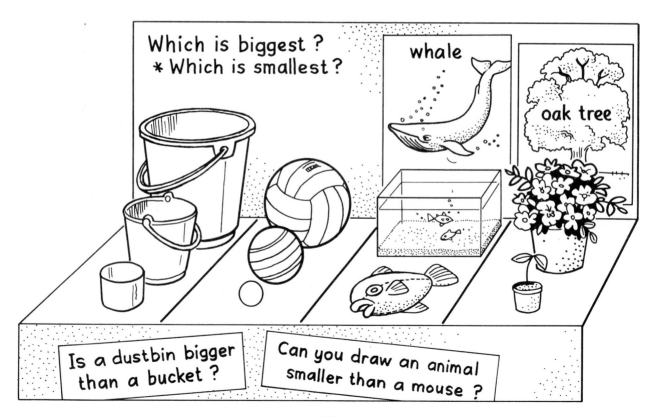

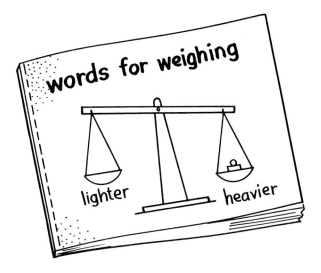

Activity 5: What is it worth?
Let the children look at money under a magnifier, and talk about and compare real coins and notes (from your purse!). Let them compare these with the play money they use for their money work at school. Look at the value written on each coin and lay them out in order.

Activity 3: How much will it hold?
Play with sand and water provides opportunities to talk about the following:

- How much? How many fill . . . ? full/empty
- more/most, less/least.

Class charts or folders will help children to recognise, use and later record the appropriate vocabulary.

Activity 4: Hot or cold?
Use the weather and how we feel, what we and our pets do in summer and winter, and a collection of objects including, for example, a warm drink, a hot water bottle with warm water in it, and metal or stone which is cold to the touch. Talk about hot and cold and establish the vocabulary of temperature, including:

- hot/hotter/hottest, cold/colder/coldest
- warm/warmer/warmest, cool/cooler/coolest.

Add these words to the class measures folder.

Activity 6: Early or late?
The school day can be a starting point for talk about time and timing, including:

- school times, kinds of clocks, clock face, hands, timing in sport
- early/earlier/earliest, late/later/latest
- before/after, hours/o'clock.

Annotated clock books are useful additions to the book corner.

Activity 7: How hard/flexible/transparent/recyclable is it?
Assemble a variety of materials which the children can handle and make judgements about. Their observations do not need to be exhaustive, but they should get plenty of practice in making comparisons. You could include, for example, wool, stone, plastic, wood, newspaper, chalk, metal, cotton fabric and cardboard.

| Area of study 17 | P of S 4a | LD 1 | **COMPARE AND ORDER** | C 90, 91 |

Commentary

This work can follow on from or tie in with 'Talking about measures' above.

As with number, start with the children themselves. They are the most readily available resource, and will be motivated when they are both learner and teaching aid. Be sensitive to the children's feelings about their characteristics. To be the shortest or to have the biggest family or ears in the group may be embarrassing to a child. Think before you encourage the children to make these comparisons.

Note that we have put 'weight' in quotation marks, because what we measure in this way is actually mass. We shall, however, use the word 'weight' as it is what we say in everyday speech.

Activity 1: Ourselves

Let the children make comparisons between one another. Invite three children of differing heights to stand in front of the others and ask the rest to call out in answer to, for example: 'Who is the tallest?' (Hal)

Hal   Tony   Charlene

fence

classroom

Mrs Turner's bike

skipping rope

'Who is the shortest?' (Tony) 'How many people are taller than Charlene?' (One, Hal) 'Who is wearing the longest sleeves?' (Tony) 'Who has the most buttons?' (Charlene) Compare the children's hair length. (Charlene's is the longest, Hal's the shortest. Tony's hair is longer than Hal's and shorter than Charlene's. Two people have hair shorter than Charlene's. Two people have hair longer than Hal's. And so on).

Compare a variety of characteristics, choosing two, three or more children for the comparisons. You could compare, for example:

● hair, noses, ears, eyes, specs
● sleeves, collars, buttons, lengths of skirts or trousers
● shoe sizes, hand sizes.

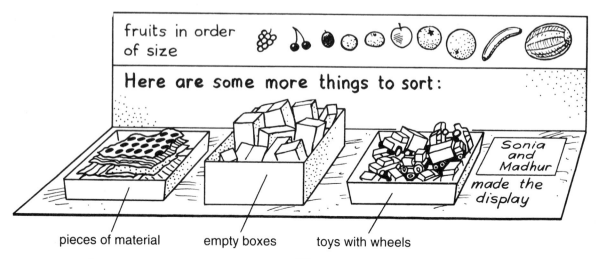

fruits in order of size

Here are some more things to sort:

Sonia and Madhur made the display

pieces of material   empty boxes   toys with wheels

Activity 2: Things around us
Try to bring in as wide a range of things as possible for comparisons, including things smaller than a shirt button (perhaps an apple pip or honesty seed), covering more ground than the classroom (perhaps the hall or playing field), longer than a skipping rope (maybe the school fence!) and bigger than the head-teacher's car (perhaps the swimming coach or minibus).

Arrange comparison displays in the classroom and let all the children contribute and take turns at arranging them, or deciding the comparisons.

Copymaster 90 (Measuring vocabulary) offers a simple record of some comparisons.

Activity 3: Things we know about
Invite the children to make more comparisons on the basis of information about themselves and their friends – for example (even if they boast!), the sizes of their appetites, their bedtimes, and the sizes of their pets are all starting points for comparisons.

Copymaster 91 (Comparing measurements) allows a record of some comparisons between a child and two friends.

Ellie, Angela and Win compared their pets		
Angela's pony **'Star'** is biggest	Win's hamster **'Blotch'** is smallest	Ellie's cat **'Toots'** is smaller than **'Star'** and bigger than **'Blotch'**

Area of study	P of S	LD		
18	4a	1	**PLAYING MEASURING**	C 92

Commentary
Role play is discussed in the section on number. We have used the same settings here to give children specific experience of measures.

Activity 1: Play house
Size play may include a comparison with things in children's own homes, in the play house and in a dolls' house. The three bears can inhabit the play house for a few days while the children assemble, order and compare all their belongings. If the class does not have three bears as resources, make them out of card. They can be made to stand in the house and have paper clothes put on them like paper dolls.

The children can set out the bears' bowls, beds, spoons, paw prints and other characteristics.

Time play may include a list of 'jobs' to do in the house, with discussion of 'before' and 'after'. The dolls could have a play timetable, devised and carried through by the children.

Activity 2: Play shop or restaurant
The play shop can have a range of contents, for example like those we mentioned in the section on number. Another possibility which may give a range of learning opportunities is a restaurant. Here are some ideas to set the business going:

● Size of plate, portion, table, cloth
● Capacity of teapot, jug, cup, glass, bottle (all plastic)
● 'Weight' of meat in burger (the children may know about quarter pounders) or steak.

Dad Baby Mum

clothes for the Teds

99

The 'customers' could comment on the food, either in a group discussion or on paper. This may be their first recording of comparisons. The comment sheet could say, for example, 'Draw what you had to eat. Was it less (or more) than you eat at home? Are the portions smaller (or bigger) than you like?' Display the children's comments and suggestions, highlighting all the measurement vocabulary they are using.

This work can be dramatised to make part of an entertaining assembly.

Copymaster C92 (Restaurant comments) is a 'customer comments' sheet for the restaurant.

Activity 3: Play post office
A play post office gives opportunities for playing with coins, and comparing the weights of parcels.

Activity 4: Play spaceship
Equip your spaceship for a two-day trip. Collect empty packets, cans, bottles, wrappers, etc. 'How much food and drink will you need to take? How much luggage space will it take up? Can the space travellers fit in too?'

Area of study 19	P of S 4a	LD 2	STARTING TO MEASURE	C93 -95

Commentary
The intention here is to give the children a wide range of practical experiences in measuring things themselves, and in beginning to record what they have measured.

The important point to get across to the children is that measuring has to be done carefully.

Estimation is as important in measurement as it is in number work. Note that estimation involving liquids can be more difficult than work with solids.

Activity 1: Handspans, cubits, feet and strides
Show the children how to measure length using their own personal measures, for example, handspans, cubits, feet and strides. You may also wish to give the children practice in using thumbs, fingers, books, pencils, blocks and other things from the maths resource box to measure length (and breadth and height).

Discuss with the children the idea of choosing the unit used to measure, basing the decision on an estimate of the outcome. For example, we may choose to measure across a room in strides, rather than pencils.

Here are some suggestions for tasks to give the children and some of the possible measuring 'units' they may use:

- Room, carpet, corridor, number line – strides, paces, feet
- Cupboard, window, table, wallchart, curtains – handspans, cubits

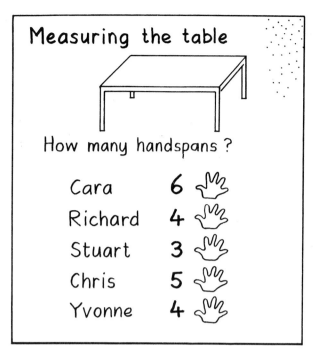

Measuring the table

How many handspans?

Cara	6
Richard	4
Stuart	3
Chris	5
Yvonne	4

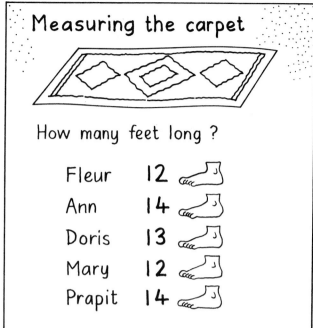

Measuring the carpet

How many feet long?

Fleur	12
Ann	14
Doris	13
Mary	12
Prapit	14

● Books, charts, pictures – fingers, blocks, pencils.

Draw the children's attention to the fact that they do not all get the same answers in their measuring. Set out some of the measurements children have made as a resource/display.

Enliven the measurement tasks by doing a couple of tasks involving the whole class. For example, find out how many children need to lie head to toe to fit across the hall, and how many feet are needed to cross the room.

You may also supply the children with some exciting shapes to use for their measuring, including, for example, toy snakes or cardboard dragons. **Copymaster 93** (Exciting things to measure with) can be copied on to card and the shapes cut out and used for measuring.

Copymaster 94 (Measuring: non-standard units) gives the children opportunities to record their measuring.

cartons will cover a chair seat, and how many matchboxes will cover a word book. Let the children set their own tasks in finding 'how many... cover a...' Compile a class book for the reading corner.

Activity 3: Play at estimating measures

Give the children opportunities to make estimates in measurement. Here are some suggestions:

● How many exercise books cover your table?
● How many strides does it take to cross the classroom?
● How many 'feet' is it across the carpet?
● How many thumbs fit across the register?
● How many bricks will fit in the shoe box with its lid on?
● How many toy sheep will fit in the sheep pen (standing up)?

Activity 2: Covering with books, cartons and blocks

Begin work on area by asking the children what they think area is. Play at estimating; for example, how many books will cover the carpet, how many cornflake

area book

It takes **8** books to cover the table

It takes **15** children to cover the carpet

Activity 4: Weighing with Plasticine®, blocks and Multilink®

Assemble a weighing table complete with balls of Plasticine®, wooden blocks and Multilink®, and a tray of things to weigh. Set a number of practical tasks which the children can do in turn. They can then complete their own weighing tasks and picture record.

Activity 5: Jugfuls and mugfuls

Structure the children's water play by setting them estimating and measuring tasks, using a variety of containers. When they are adept at the practical work, let them begin to record their findings and then set them problems.

Copymaster 95 (Capacity) poses some problems which the children can try to solve.

Activity 6: Who is quicker?

Try timing by counting. Ask a child to count while another child jumps up and down 20 times. Let the children invent their own 'timing' methods. They could include measuring tasks like these:

● Holding their breath
● Reading a page of a book aloud
● Recalling ten colours
● Doing a simple jigsaw.

As timing devices children could use chalk marks on a board, cuts in paper, drops into a box using a building block, or other things that the children can devise.

Try making sand clocks and water clocks and using these as timing devices. For example, the children could set each other tasks to do while one scoop of sand runs through the timer, or while the water clock drips ten droplets.

Sand clock

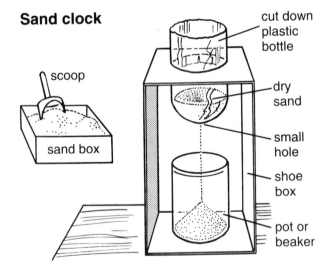

Water clock

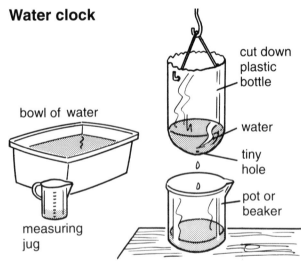

Area of study 20	P of S 4a	LD 2

WHY WE AGREE ON MEASURES TO USE ▶

Commentary

Only when children understand the need for standard measures can they begin to appreciate just how carefully measurement must be done; thus it is important to discuss standard measures.

Activity: Comparing results

Assemble some of the children's results from the previous activities under 'Starting to measure' and let the children look at them carefully. Record their discussion on tape, or write up the important points they make. They should be able to make connections, for example, between the size of their hands and the number of handspans each of them takes to measure a table. This is the point at which to begin to introduce standard measures.

Area of study 21	P of S 4a	LD 2

COMMON STANDARD MEASURES

Commentary

When metric measures (particularly decimal currency) were introduced to Britain, many teachers began to teach small children metric units only. The pace of change was grossly over-estimated and we are still using feet and yards, square yards, pints, pounds and ounces. As these are in common use, children need to know about them and be able to use them.

The introduction of different kinds of measuring units to measure similar things requires careful planning and sensitivity. Explain a metric measure in a different session from an imperial one. Let the children carry metric or imperial measures through a piece of work.

Once the children have been introduced to standard measures, encourage them to make estimates before they try to measure and get an answer. It is important that they should have an idea of what a metre looks or feels like, so that they can predict the 'order' of their answer.

Activity 1: Standard measures of length, width and breadth

In separate sessions show the children metre sticks, school rulers, tapes and spring rules. Let them create a set of homemade resources for measuring, including cardboard metre strips and string or 'tape' measures a metre long. Important units to cover in these sessions include metres and yards. Also discuss miles and kilometres with the children.

Activity 3: Standard measures of 'weight'

Show children a pair of kitchen scales and bathroom scales. Discuss pounds and kilograms.

Area of study 22	P of S 4a	LD 3

STANDARD MEASURES

C96 –101

Commentary

At Level 2 the children were introduced to some common imperial and metric measures. They can now begin to work with the other metric units in general use, like the gram and centimetre.

Now that the children will attempt measurement in small units, it is even more important to stress the need for carefulness.

Activity 1: A centimetre rule

Show the children that a metre can be cut into 100 equal pieces, each piece being called a centimetre. Give the children card strips a metre long with centimetre divisions, and let them mark on the numerals. They can use this strip to measure around the classroom and school.

Copymaster 96 (Measuring in centimetres) gives same practice.

When the children are proficient at measuring they can apply this skill in other areas of the curriculum including technology and art. For example, they can measure some material and make glove puppets.

Activity 2: Pints, litres and millilitres

Let the children fill, empty and decant the contents of a milk bottle to establish what a pint looks like.

We buy fruit juice in litres, and milk is sold in supermarkets in litres. Examine some packaging and containers with the children to see what is measured in litres. Let the children do cooking, and use metric measures, and on other occasions imperial measures.

Copymaster 97 (Litres and millilitres) gives practice in measuring millilitres.

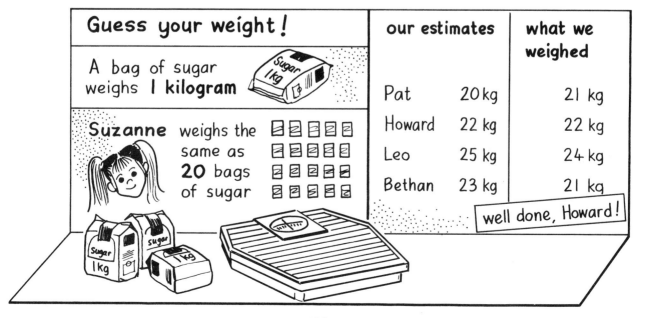

Look at and compare these little bags of food

| 10g rice | 5g coconut | 20g beans | 2g tea | 50g barley | 30g pasta | 2g spice |
| 1g herbs | 5g tea | 3g oats | 20g pasta | 10g coffee | 20g sugar | 5g rice |

Activity 3: Weighing in kilograms and grams

Sugar is commonly sold in kilogram bags, so a full bag would give children an idea of how a kilogram feels. They can then estimate how much they themselves weigh and test their estimates on some bathroom scales. Help the children to tabulate their results.

Pack in sealed transparent plastic bags 1 gram, 2 grams, 3 grams, 5 grams and 10 grams of some common foodstuffs. You could include, for example, uncooked pasta, semolina, dessicated coconut, raw oats, loose tea, spice, herbs, dried beans, rice and barley. Arrange these in a display so that the children can freely handle them and compare them.

Let the children use a classroom balance to weigh some things from the mathematics resource box. Pre-select some items to ensure a range of experience. Let the children compare the results they obtain. They should all agree – discuss the possible reasons for any discrepancies. Depending on the construction of the balance, discuss with the children the kinds of things that can be weighed easily on it and its optimum range in terms of 'weight'. If you can, let the children look closely at other kinds of weighing machine, like a letter scales, a spring balance, and those the school nurse uses, and discuss their likely ranges.

Use an accurate kitchen balance in cooking, and let the children do the weighing.

Activity 4: Measuring time

The standard measures of time will be more familiar to the children than some other standard measures. However, the fact that they talk about bedtimes and

On Tuesday we had a time check day

* at 9 o'clock we were doing Register
* at 10 o'clock we were doing Maths and Art
* at 11 o'clock we were in Assembly
* at 12 o'clock we stopped for lunch

We spent 3 hours in school on Tuesday morning

The story of our Tuesday morning

Maths measures and sums | paper butterflies | out to play | Assembly our prayer | some good writing

104

being late for school does not mean that they have an understanding of time. To give them a sense of an hour, you could have a 'time check' day, where you begin by 'clocking the children in', discuss with them the total amount of time there is in the school day and what your plans are for their activities. Each hour (or half hour) have a time check, and tell the children how much of the school day has passed.

Tell the children about the vocabulary of time, and about 12- and 24-hour clocks.

You can play 'What is a minute?' by asking the children to close their eyes, put up a hand, and then take it down when they think a minute has passed. Introduce a minute into music and rhythm work. With a minute timer, pairs of children can set each other a range of challenges, including some of the following. How many times in a minute can you:

- write your name
- sing 'Jack and Jill'
- run round the hall
- hop across the carpet
- blink your eyes
- touch your toes . . .

A second is a good time interval for banging a drum, hopping or jumping, playing maraccas, tapping your foot, stamping, winking and doing a quick repertoire of actions like you find in some machines.

Activity 5: Play hospital
There are a variety of role play settings in which children can work on measures. Here is an example.

Real weighing and measuring can be introduced into the 'health clinic'. The children can use height measures, scales and foot measures to determine and compare data about each other, for example:

Height in cm
Weight in kilograms and grams
Foot size.

Data can be used to make comparisons, draw graphs and test hypotheses. For example:

- Do the tallest people in the class have the biggest feet?
- Is the average height for the boys taller than for the girls?

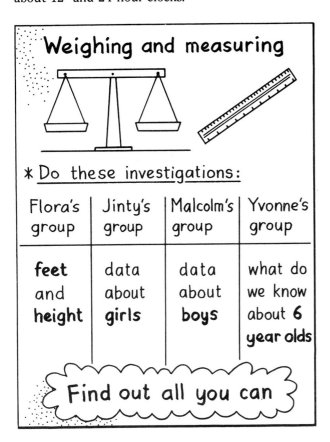

Weighing and measuring

* Do these investigations:

Flora's group	Jinty's group	Malcolm's group	Yvonne's group
feet and **height**	data about **girls**	data about **boys**	what do we know about **6 year olds**

Find out all you can

Draw the hands to show **half past nine**

The time is
_____
_____

Here are **2 clocks**

What is the **time difference**?

This clock has no long hand. Can you still tell the time?

● Do the girls' foot sizes have a bigger range than the boys?

Ideas about temperature and pulse rate can be introduced.

Activity 6: Telling the time

Children do need to be told exactly what happens to the hands on a clock, and how to tell the time from it. An enormous clock face, with every minute marked, the quarters and half past, and arabic numerals for the numbers helps. There is a small clock face on **copymaster 98** to which the children can add hands.

Make a game of reading the clock face. Use a play clock and do oral work to enable children to learn from one another. Here are some of the written presentations which you can use to give the children plenty of practice with conventional clocks.

● Clock face with time written in – child puts in hands
● Clock face with hands – child writes the time
● Two clock faces with hands – child works out time difference

● Clock face with long hand missing – child writes in time.

Tie in work on the hour with the children's daily routine. The quarter and half hours may sometimes tally with playtimes and assembly times. Collect these significant times and display them.

Set challenges like 'In an hour's time what will the clock say?' 'The minute hand has fallen off this clock. Can we still use it to tell the time?'

Copymaster 99 (Telling the time) includes some time puzzles.

Look at digital times too. A cardboard number rest with a box of small cards with numerals on them and a card with a point or two points on it can be used to set up times.

Make a display where the children can come and set the hands on a clock, change the digital time, match the clock to the classroom clock, and put on the clock lunchtime, playtime, lighting-up time, high tide, the time of the next train to the city and other times important in your community.

Copymaster 100 (Digital/written time) and **101** (Time) give the children opportunities for some practice work on time.

ESTIMATING MEASUREMENTS

Area of study **23** | P of S **4a** | LD **3**

Commentary

Estimation is an integral part of the mastery of measurement. Without the ability to estimate, the children will not be able to solve measuring problems or cope with measures in life. It is therefore very important to let the children make estimates as often as is feasible.

Estimation in measurement, as in most mathematical work with children, is difficult to teach. One reason for this is the emphasis that we place in mathematics teaching on accuracy. From the child's viewpoint, on the one hand we are asking for the production of the one right answer but on the other we ask for a set of best guesses. It is important, therefore, to help children to see estimation as an integral part of the process at arriving at solutions which are good enough in the given circumstances. For example, while we need to estimate the whole number of rolls of wallpaper we need for decorating (and we know that some will be

left over), we need a more precise solution to cutting a length of wood to make a shelf.

Activity: Estimating measurements

As soon as the children have been introduced to a measure, they can start to use it in their estimations. When you set them problems, ask them to make an estimate before they measure. Give them oral problems to solve. For example:

● Could a giant a metre wide get through the classroom door?
● How much water do the fish need in the aquarium if they are used to a minimum depth of 20 cm?
● How does the 'weight' of 10 pencils compare with that of 10 crayons?
● How many times can you count in twos to 20 in a minute?

There are endless possibilities.

CONSERVATION OF MEASURES

Commentary

Position and orientation are vital to the ability to conserve measures. Link measuring activities the children do to their work in PE, dance and shape, in order that study in one area will support understanding in others.

Conservation of a wide variety of measures in a range of situations is only achievable through practical experience. If, for example, you have tried cooking in someone else's kitchen, only to find that the pots seem to be all the wrong shapes and sizes, you will know that adults cannot conserve capacity in unfamiliar settings! The children's confidence in conserving measures will be directly related, therefore, to the breadth of the range of different measuring situations they have worked in.

Activity: Conservation discussion and demonstration

In discussion, present the children with a series of situations in which the conservation of measurement is clear. Here are a few starter examples:

● A teacher's table is the same length on every day of the week!

● We cannot lengthen a curtain by taking some off the top and adding it to the bottom.

● One bottle full of milk will make two, three or even ten drinks but there is still no more than a bottle full.

● An unopened bag of flour weighs the same on any scales, at any time (provided the scales are accurate!).

You can demonstrate conservation, but remember that evidence that the children can conserve in one situation is not necessarily generalisable to others.

Programme of study: Shape, space and measures

Pupils should be taught to:

■ **4. Understanding and using measures**

b choose and use simple measuring instruments, reading and interpreting numbers and scales with some accuracy.

CHOOSING AND USING INSTRUMENTS

Commentary

If the children have had a wide range of practical experiences in measuring, they themselves will now be able to decide which instrument to use for which measuring job.

Once the children start to use standard measures, all their measuring work is 'action' based and like 'real life'. We have therefore not attempted to set up role play situations but suggest instead a series of projects which will take the children into an investigation of real measures.

Try to alert the children to all the incidental learning opportunities, by, for example, looking at the sizing on Dana's new coat and discussing how and where it is measured, and what size shoes most children have.

Activity 1: How to measure investigations

Set some open-ended investigations which children can do alone and in twos. Here are some possibilities:

a) Pretend you are building a new hutch for a rabbit, or cage for a budgie. Decide on the materials, the approximate size, the tools you would need

(including measuring tools), the units you would do your measuring in and what you would need to know about the rabbit. List all these things, and do a sketch of how the hutch will look.

b) You are the designer of a bench seat for two children to sit on. What measuring tools do you need, and what do you need to know about the children?

c) Find out how long it takes for everyone to come in from the playground, after the whistle has blown. What did you use to do your measurements? Could you have measured it in some other way?

d) A good way to make pastry is to add to the bowl half as much fat as you have flour. Make some pastry using 80 grams of fat. How much flour do you need? Rub the mixture until it looks like fine breadcrumbs, and then add a tiny amount of water, so that you can make a dough. Roll it out $\frac{1}{2}$ cm thick and cut into 8 cm circles. Put in a patty pan, add a little jam to each. Ask an adult to put them in a hot oven for 10 minutes. How many tarts did you make? What would you need to make twice as many?

e) What is the difference in 'weight' between the lightest and the heaviest person in the class? What did you use to make the measurements? (Be careful of children's sensitivities if you set this project.)

Activity 2: Projects using measures

a) Interview a school architect about some of the things they take into account when designing a school. Discuss with them the children's ideas about how their current school design could be changed to better accommodate children of primary age. For example, the children could ask for window sills not to stick out at eye level, display boards not to be $1\frac{1}{2}$ metres off the ground, and corridors to the playground to be wider.

b) Discuss with the children the optimum size for a desk, working surface, or exercise book. They will have opinions about working in too small a space or on paper that gets scuffed at the corners. They could make their own books to match their ideals. Discuss the dimensions of pens, pencils and crayons for ease of handling and working. For example, manufacturers produce 'fat' crayons and thick brushes for small hands. Do the children themselves find these easier to work with?

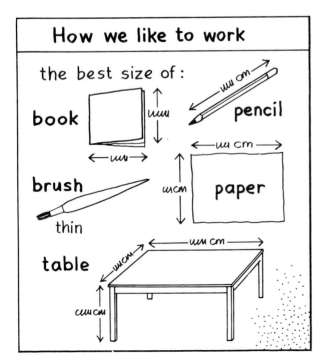

c) Do a classroom temperature check (the children may not be ready to read the thermometer themselves (see Science AT 3 Level 4) so you can read it and band the recordings cold . . . cool . . . warm . . . too warm). Ask a sample of children how they find the temperature. Ask those same children to report on how they felt when they first went outside to play. Discuss and display the results.

d) Ask the school doctor or nurse to talk to the children about our fluid needs. They can say what a baby needs, what we need every day, and which drinks are healthy.

e) Ask the officials at the local swimming pool to give you some details about the dimensions of the pools, how much water they hold, how often they are cleaned and what is added to the water.

f) If there is a reservoir near the school, ask the officials there for the statistics about it. How much does it hold? How much water does it take for it to rise 1 cm? How many people get their water from it? How much water does a family use in a day?

g) Let the children prepare food and drinks and do cooking to produce healthy food, and have practice in measuring out liquids and weighing ingredients.

h) Visit a post office and look at the letter scales and parcel scales. Look at the cost of sending letters and parcels of different weights.

i) Make a variety of clocks, using sand, water, candles (close supervision required) and make sundials with the children (see Science AT 4 Level 3). Examine the inside of a conventional wind-up clock to see how it works. Ask a local watch-mender or clock enthusiast to tell the children the main components of a clock (this will help their understanding of gears and levers). Look at railway and bus timetables and discuss the use of the 24-hour clock.

j) Investigate the use of timers in sport. Look at world records. Look at speedometers and trip meters on bicycles and in cars and discuss how we read them. Investigate speed limits.

Any of the above investigations could form the starting points for a topic, work for a display, open evening or assembly.

RECORD SHEET

Name _____

AT	Level 1	Level 2	Level 3
1			
2			
3			

Name _____

AT2 Number	1	2	3	4
	5	6	7	8
	9	10	11	12
	13	14	15	16
	17	18	19	20
	21	22	23	24
	25	26	27	28
	29	30	31	32
	33	34	35	36
	37	38	39	40
	41	42	43	44
	45	46	47	48
	49	50	51	52
	53	54	55	56
	57	58	59	60
	61	62	63	64
	65	66	67	68
	69			
AT3 Shape, space and measures	70	71	72	73
	74	75	76	77
	78	79	80	81
	82	83	84	85
	86	87	88	89
	90	91	92	93
	94	95	96	97
	98	99	100	101